Sophie
Nina
Danielle
Simon
Ben
Thomas
Nicola
Heather
Luke
Ross

C000065123

Spane people

come not Inst.

# Sophie

will you come to my DISCO

s.
Remember it on the 13th February 99
might be cold from 6:00pm till 9:00pm
so bring a At my house
jacket or
coat. In the Garage

Rs

Michelle

I will be / I won't be
coming / able to make it

from

Sophie

front

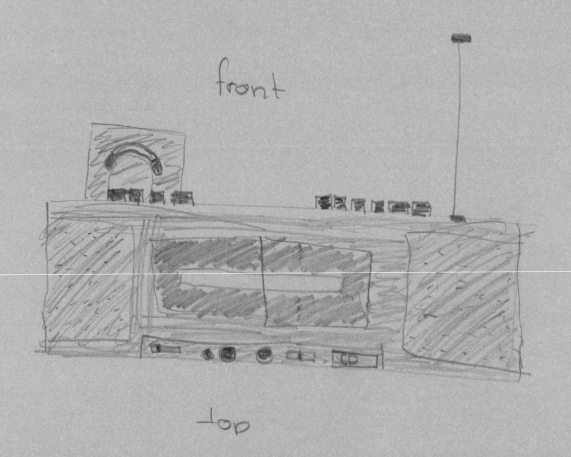

top

# KIDS PARTY Book

Illustrations by Gaye C. Chapman

**LEOPARD**

# Contents

T HIS BOOK offers you exciting ideas for fifteen different theme parties, with many variations. For each party, we suggest the suitable age group, venue and number of guests; give ideas for invitations, decorations, games and prizes; suggest a menu and a party cake, and provide tempting recipes. Following the theme parties are more recipes for favourite party fare, basic cakes and frostings, as well as an excellent section on all sorts of games — traditional, quiet, active — suitable for group or individual play.

---

COOKERY RATING

Easy: simple to make
Medium: a little more skill needed
Advanced: for confident cooks

# *Party Planning*

*Vampire Blood* (see page 47)

*Fairy Bread* (see page 94)

*Moon Buggy Wheels* (see page 55)

D O YOU HAVE A CHILD'S PARTY coming up? A little forward planning will help to turn the day into a memorable occasion. Parties can be small-scale fun or grand-scale productions. The best parties are often the most simple, and a little creative effort will go a long way to ensuring a successful, hassle-free event.

A particular theme can add lots of fun to a party for any age group. A theme can be the springboard for more ideas on decorations and food — as well as invitations, cake, games, prizes and guests' clothing. A party theme is a good starting point for planning, and adds interest all round.

## WHEN, WHERE AND WHO

The first step in planning any party is deciding where it is to be held. There are so many options: the home, garden, park, zoo, amusement park, bowling centre, restaurant, theatre, cinema, pop concert, beach, swimming pool or boat. Your area may offer a special venue, in or out of doors. Ask your local council for information if you are new to the neighbourhood. A particular hobby could suggest a venue; a picnic and riding party could be held at a local riding school, for example.

The venue, day and length of the party will determine the number of guests you can accommodate, afford and deal with. It makes things easier if some of the invited children know one another. Your child, as the host, should draw up the guest list. Even very young children have firm ideas on whom they want to invite. If you can't cope with a large number, say so at the beginning, and give your child a number to work with — for example, 6 or 10. A small group of happy children can form the basis of a terrific party. A large party, consisting of different age groups, not familiar with each other, can separate into small fragments and will be harder to organise for games.

## FOOD, THEMES AND FUN

Having chosen the venue, step two is the all-important choice of the type of food to be served. The venue can dictate the menu. At home, or in your garden, it is easy to have traditional party fare with all the trimmings. It helps to keep the food away from the play area, in another room or a different corner of the garden. Try (not always easy) to serve the food as an event on its own.

For parties at outdoor venues, such as the park, beach, or riding school, the food should be simpler and easy to transport. Parties held in restaurants offer the easiest food option, but can be expensive.

Zoos, amusement parks and bowling centres often cater for parties and will give you special rates. If you are taking the children to the theatre, cinema or a pop concert, remember to plan for a time to provide party food and the cake. If transport is a problem, plan for the closest venue — the nearest park, or restaurant. Alternatively, have a mock dinner party at home.

Whether you take the children out to eat, or have the party at home, remember the magic ingredient itself — the cake. A party's not a party without one. Always supply plenty to

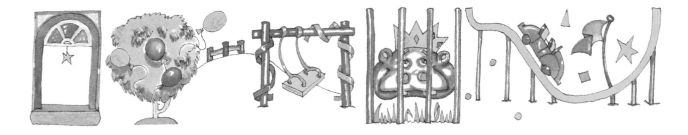

drink. Child's play is thirsty work, and children consume large quantities at parties. In fact, they often drink more than they eat.

Some children react badly to artificial food colourings and sweeteners. In a party of very young children, check with other parents that there are no food allergies.

To ensure that you relax, enjoy yourself and pass on a happy feeling, a couple of good helpers (or more if the guests are very young) will be a valuable asset on the day.

Party games are usually voted the best part of the entertainment and children love them. Step three of your plan is to draw up a list of games. Think about when to start them, about what time you plan to serve the food and cut the cake. The programme for games should be varied — 10 minutes is usually long enough for most games. Find all the equipment you need for each game well before the guests arrive — thimbles, scarves for blindfolds and so on. Your written list will help you keep an eye on the time and your programme and keep things moving. It helps to be flexible. If a particular game is a roaring success, let it run on for a while, in place of the next one on the list.

Pages 102 to 110 contain lots of ideas for a variety of games, from the traditional to the new, to suit all ages.

If you have chosen a theme for the party, try not to get too carried away with fancy dress ideas. Choose themes with which parents are going to be able to cope. Many parents are very busy and can't sit up for two nights at the sewing machine making a costume. Try not to make dressing up too competitive — some parents will head for the nearest hire service, while others won't be able to afford it and their children will feel their outfits aren't good enough.

Consider what might be easy. If most guests or their parents are keen horse-riders or hikers, an equestrian or camping party will present no problems. Beach clothes can make cheap and colourful outfits. Children who go to martial art classes will immediately have a costume for a judo or Japanese party. You'll find a selection of themes later on in this book, all of which can offer you a whole party plan, or can be adapted to suit your own particular group.

## INVITATIONS

Written invitations are fun for all age groups. Children love to receive them. They give essential information to parents, and provide definite arrival and departure times. Parents transporting young children will appreciate having your telephone number close to hand.

Make or buy the party invitations, and send them about two weeks in advance. The best invitations are often handmade. Design yours so that they reflect the type of party it will be — a clown shape for a clown party, for example. Coloured card is inexpensive and easily found.

Stationery stores sell attractive invitations with blank spaces for filling in the time, place, and date. There is usually a large selection of invitations; you're almost certain to find the one that fits your kind of party.

Remember to include start and finish times, your street address — add a small map on the back of the card if your street is hard to find — and add your telephone number. Include any special information such as what to wear, or alternative

*Exciting decoration sets the mood for a Disco Party* (page 86)

arrangements in case of rain. It's useful to ask guests or their parents to R.S.V.P., so that you have a clear idea of the numbers of guests to expect.

## THEMES, TRIMMINGS AND PARTY IDEAS

All of the suggested themes in this book can be adapted to suit your own special requirements and imagination. If your time is limited, don't try to make everything for the party — all the food, the cake, invitations, outfits, decorations, as well as organising the games. Do what you are best at, like making the cake and food, then buy the decorations and invitations. Get the children involved and ask a friend or two to help on the day.

## SWEETS

Once children start to visit other people's homes or go to pre-school, they soon discover the delights of sweets, ice-creams and salty things in packets. Most children love sweet things and expect them at parties.

If there is a health reason for sweets not being allowed, or if you prefer not to offer them, there are other delicious and healthy alternatives. Small boxes of sultanas, raisins, dried apples or apricots are popular with most children, so are dried banana chips and unsalted peanuts.

Sweets tied up in bags are a favourite take-home party favour and chocolate bars are acceptable inexpensive prizes. On pages 98 to 101 you will find tempting and attractive suggestions for sweets and candies.

## BALLOONS

Balloons are a must for any party, whatever the age. Tie a few to the gate or doorknocker to make your house easy to find. Colourful and cheap, balloons give a boost to all decorations regardless of the theme, and children love taking them home afterwards. Try to have plenty of spares on hand to replace the ones which burst just as the children are about to leave.

Don't think you can forget the balloons just because the party is outdoors. In a large field or park, a bunch of balloons tied to the nearest tree makes your group easy to spot. Get the children to blow them up before the party or have a balloon-blowing contest. If you want to use hundreds for a big event, use a lilo or air bed pump.

Helium balloons are fun and can be obtained from speciality shops. Party shops sell a range of shapes and colours of balloons, as well as the skinny-sausage variety which can be twisted and shaped into animals or initials for that extra touch.

Very small children may be startled by balloons bursting, and will need comforting. Remember, too, that children — even older ones — should not put pieces of burst balloon in their mouths as they can easily choke.

## FANCY DRESS

Crêpe paper is a wonderful stand-by for decorating or making a fancy dress. It's cheap and can be tied, stitched, stapled, or pinned. It can be used in almost any theme; it will make a dramatic cape for a vampire, a cloth and a deep frill to encircle a table, or a flower-petal hat.

Felt is another fantastic fabric for making a quick fancy dress, or for decorating existing clothes with cut-out stars, letters or stripes. It needs only to be tacked on, for easy removal after the party. It can also be glued to

*Card, glitter and balloons add a festive touch to the Space Party* (page 50)

cardboard or other surfaces. Available in a multitude of colours from most haberdashery departments, it has the added advantage of being cheap. Do remember, though, to remove felt additions from ordinary clothes afterwards, before putting the clothes in the wash. Felt colours, like those of crêpe paper, do run.

Paper streamers, available from most supermarkets, add a festive touch, as do party hats, masks and tooters. Party hats or masks can also be made to enhance a theme. Most stationers have a range of light card or coloured paper. Add glue, staples, hat elastic and a sprinkling of glitter, and you can create a cast of thousands.

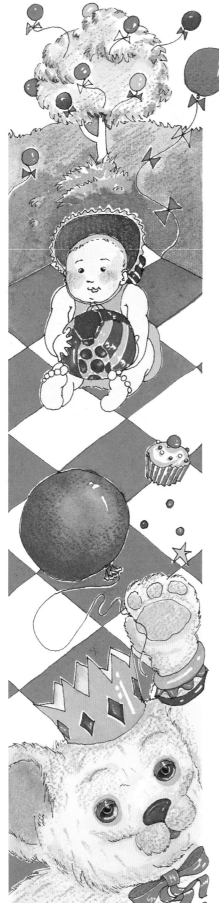

# First Party

I T IS HARD to resist having a party for your baby's first birthday, even if the child is not aware of the occasion. It provides a pleasant opportunity to spend the day with other new mothers. Grandparents often want to attend. Keep it simple. Pick a shady spot in the park and spread out the picnic blankets.

**Age group:** one
**Venue:** park or botanical garden
**Number of guests:** minimal

**Invitations**
Invite guests by telephone, or a card with a large 'one', a single candle or any other card you can find suggesting 'one'.

**Decorations**
Bright and colourful plastic picnic ware is best, as paper plates and cups get knocked over too easily and can be chewed. Tie a bunch of balloons to a tree to mark your picnic spot, but keep the balloons out of reach of babies, and be prepared to comfort those who are frightened by a bursting balloon.

**Food**
Check with other mothers which foods they have introduced. Most babies of this age will eat biscuits, yoghurt, jelly and cup cakes. For the mums and older children, have French bread, a few good cheeses, suitable dips and pieces of fruit. Drumsticks are easy to carry and are a savoury welcome to most adults at a child's party, but remember to remove the splinter bone and cartilage before giving one to a baby to gnaw.

**Cake:** a Gingham Dog cake is simple to make.

**Games**
Bring along soft rubber or fabric balls or rattles for each baby. A packet of

colourful plastic bangles will amuse them. Have plenty of safe toys on hand. When babies tire, prams or strollers will provide a soothing change and give you the opportunity for a walk in the park.

**Party Favours**
The soft balls and plastic bangles you brought along.

## GINGHAM DOG CAKE

*Preparation time:* 50 minutes
*Cooking time:* 40 minutes
*Easy*

1 x 350 g packet cake mix or one
    quantity of butter cake batter
    (see page 96)
2 quantities butter icing (see page 96)
green food colouring
Smarties for decoration

1. Preheat oven to 180°C. Grease and line an 18 x 28 cm shallow tin. Make the cake according to directions on the packet or recipe. Pour mixture

into prepared tin and bake for 35–40 minutes or until cooked. Cool.

2. Cut cake into sections as shown in diagram. Discard shaded pieces and assemble pieces as shown, joining the pieces with a little butter icing.

3. Divide remaining icing in half and use one half to cover the top and sides of the cake. Leave to set. Using a ruler and a fine skewer, prick lines on the dog's body, dividing it into squares (see photograph).

4. Tint remaining icing green or another colour. Fill an icing bag fitted with a writing tube or use a paper bag with the tip cut off. Pipe lines on the cake, following the marks, then decorate with more lines and dots as shown. Arrange Smarties to make the dog's collar, nose and eye, securing them with dabs of icing.

Gingham Dog Cake

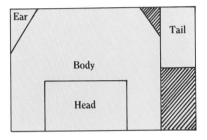

*Gingham Dog Cake*

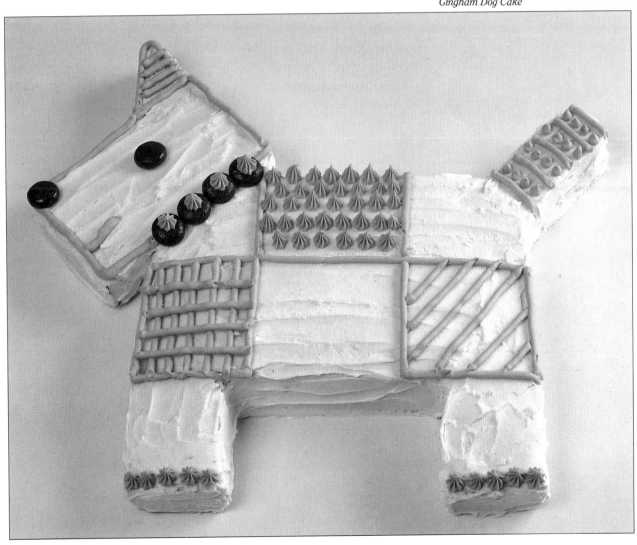

# Clown Party

THE SECOND and third birthdays are an excellent opportunity for a small-scale party. Invite other children from the neighbourhood or local playgroup. Two or three parents would be helpful, as toddlers need assistance and attention. Holding the party in the garden means that no-one has to worry about spilt drinks and allows parents to relax too. Keep the party short. Toddlers tire quickly and will probably need a nap after an hour or two of activity and social interaction in a group.

**Age group:** two or three years
**Venue:** the garden
**Number of guests:** 4–6

### Invitations
Cut out a clown-face card. Include the time, date, your address and telephone number.

### Decorations
Before the party, check that the area is childproof. Put away sharp gardening tools and other hazardous items. Garden furniture will be fine for adults: children will enjoy using a plastic plate and cup on the lawn. Tie balloons to a tree, and put up a garden umbrella if the day is hot. Have a basin of water and a few facecloths nearby.

*Clockwise from left: Cherry Crunch, Clown Faces, Baskets of Tricks, Peach Dream, Fairy Biscuits, Harlequin Dip and Number Sandwiches.*

*Basket of Tricks*

*Fairy Biscuits*

segments with grapefruit knife and reserve. Scoop out membrane, leaving orange shells intact.

3. To serve, cut jellies into cubes. Combine with orange segments, assorted fruits and marshmallows. Spoon into orange shells. Add a pretty flower to garnish. Chill before serving.

## FAIRY BISCUITS

*Preparation time:* 15 minutes
*Cooking time:* nil
*Makes about 12*
*Easy*

1 x 250 g packet plain biscuits
125 g cream cheese, softened
1 cup hundreds and thousands

1. Lay biscuits out on a board or tray, with the flat side facing upwards.
2. Spread each biscuit with a little cream cheese and sprinkle with hundreds and thousands.

## NUMBER SANDWICHES

*Preparation time:* 45 minutes
*Cooking time:* nil
*Serves 10*
*Easy*

1 loaf sliced bread
butter for spreading
fillings

1. Spread slices of bread thinly with butter. Spread 10 slices or half the loaf with filling and top with slices of buttered bread.
2. Cut sandwiches into number

### Food
Some toddlers may have special food or drink preferences: check with their parents. Suggested menu: Fairy Biscuits, Number Sandwiches, Basket of Tricks, Clown Faces, Cherry Crunch, Peach Dream, Harlequin Dip.

**Cake:** a Clown's Head cake is fun and easy to make.

### Games
Children aged two and three enjoy water and sand play. A baby bath filled with water, and with a good assortment of containers from the pot cupboard or plastics shelf, will be popular. If you haven't a sandpit, make a sand tray on the same lines: a large, shallow plastic or metal container filled with clean sand, some plastic cups, and a beach bucket, is a veritable honey-pot for small children. Group games could include *Ring-a-ring-a-rosy*; *Hide-and-seek*; *The Farmer in the dell*; *Follow-the-leader*; *On the bank, in the river*. Bubble

blowing is fun for three-year-old children. *Wobbling bunnies* is, too.

### Party Favours
Sweets or bags of dried fruit, and one or two balloons.

## BASKET OF TRICKS

*Preparation time:* 30 minutes plus chilling time
*Cooking time:* nil
*Serves 6*
*Easy*

½ x 85 g packet red jelly
½ x 85 g packet green jelly
3 oranges
assorted fresh or unsweetened canned fruits, cut up e.g. strawberries, bananas, canned peaches
6 marshmallows, cut into quarters

1. Prepare jellies, using a little less water than packet directs. Pour into small, shallow tins and refrigerate until jellies are firm.
2. Cut oranges in half, cut out fruit

shapes. Skewer each sandwich with a small flag with the individual child's name written on it.

3. Cover with plastic wrap or damp greaseproof paper to prevent sandwiches from drying out.

FILLINGS

*Egg Mayonnaise*
Mash together 7 hardboiled eggs, 3 tablespoons mayonnaise and pepper to taste. Divide mixture between 10 slices bread. Top with finely shredded lettuce.

*Carrot and Cheese*
Combine 5 finely grated carrots, 125 g finely grated cheese, 2 mashed hardboiled eggs, 1 stalk finely chopped celery and 1 tablespoon plain yoghurt or sour cream. Divide between 10 slices of bread.

*Tropical Delight*
Drain 1 x 425 g can crushed pineapple. Stand 10–15 minutes to allow all excess moisture to drain away. Combine with 1 x 100 g packet roughly chopped marshmallows, 1 cup sultanas, 1 cup shredded coconut and 4 tablespoons sour cream. Mix thoroughly and spread over 10 slices bread.

*Number Sandwiches*

*Cherry Crunch*

## CHERRY CRUNCH

*Preparation time*: 15 minutes
*Cooking time*: 10 minutes
*Makes 30*
*Easy*

30 g butter
2 tablespoons honey
2 tablespoons brown sugar
2 cups cornflakes
½ cup chopped glacé cherries

1. Preheat oven to 180°C. Line 30 deep muffin tins with paper cake cases.
2. Place butter, honey and sugar in a small pan. Heat gently until frothy. Combine cornflakes and cherries in a large mixing bowl. Stir in butter mixture and mix well.
3. Spoon into paper cake cases. Bake for 5–10 minutes. Remove from oven and cool on a wire rack.

*Peach Dream*

*Clown Faces*

## CLOWN FACES

*Preparation time:* 20 minutes
*Cooking time:* nil
*Serves 10*
*Easy*

1 litre vanilla ice-cream
10 ice-cream cones
½ cup shredded coconut
20 Smarties for eyes
10 glacé red cherries
1 licorice strap
5 small red snakes

1.  Scoop ice-cream into balls on a large flat tray. Arrange cones on top of ice-cream and place in freezer until firm.
2.  Decorate ice-cream with coconut for hair, Smarties for eyes and a cherry for each clown's nose. Cut licorice into fine strips 1 cm long and place vertically on top of and below each Smartie. Finish each face with half a red snake for the mouth. Serve at once.

## PEACH DREAM

*Preparation time:* 10 minutes
*Cooking time:* nil
*Serves 8*
*Easy*

1 x 425 g can peach slices
500 g litre vanilla ice-cream
¼ cup orange juice
few drops vanilla essence
2 cups milk, chilled
orange slices for garnish

1.  Drain peach slices and chill well. Put into a blender bowl with ice-cream, orange juice, vanilla essence and milk. Blend until smooth.
2.  Pour into tumblers and serve at once, garnished with orange slices.

## HARLEQUIN DIP

*Preparation time:* 30 minutes
*Cooking time:* nil
*Serves 10*
*Easy*

6 hardboiled eggs
2 tablespoons mayonnaise
2 tablespoons sour cream
2 tablespoons finely chopped fresh
   parsley
1 tablespoon poppy seeds
2 tablespoons finely chopped red
   capsicum
rice crackers for serving

*Harlequin Dip*

1. Mash hardboiled eggs with mayonnaise and sour cream. Lightly brush a small bowl with oil. Spoon egg mixture into bowl and pack firmly. Chill in the refrigerator for 1 hour.

2. Invert egg mould onto a flat serving plate. Cover a third of the top and sides of the egg mixture with finely chopped parsley, one third with poppy seeds and remaining third with capsicum. Press on lightly. Surround egg mixture with rice crackers to serve.

## CLOWN'S HEAD CAKE

*Preparation time:* 1½ hours
*Cooking time:* 45 minutes
*Easy*

2 x 350 g packets cake mix or
    2 quantities butter cake (see page 96)
1 quantity butter icing (see page 96)
red food colouring
blue food colouring
Smarties
1 licorice strap
1 chocolate finger biscuit
red crêpe paper
shirring elastic

1. Preheat oven to 180°C and grease two 20 cm round cake tins. Make the cakes according to directions on the packet or following recipe. Turn into prepared tins and bake for 40–45 minutes or until cooked. Cool.

2. Cut a hat and a pompom from one cake (see diagram). Use the second cake for the face.

3. Divide butter icing in half. Set aside one half to decorate the face. Divide the remaining half into thirds. Place one-third in one bowl and colour it deep red for the pompom. Place the remaining two-thirds in another bowl and colour it deep blue for the hat.

4. Ice the pompom and hat cakes red and blue respectively, covering tops and sides. Ice the face cake separately, spreading the reserved plain icing over top and sides of face.

5. To assemble: carefully place the hat in position, so the curve at the base of the hat fits into the top of the face. Place pompom on top of hat.

*Clown's Head Cake*

Cover the join between hat and face with Smarties, and use Smarties on the face for eyes and mouth. Use small strips of licorice for eyelashes and a long strip for the mouth. Cut the chocolate finger in half for the nose. Make a ruffle, using the red crêpe paper and shirring elastic, to finish the neck trim.

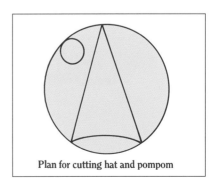

Plan for cutting hat and pompom

# ZooParty

A ZOO PARTY works well for younger children. If you have a zoo in your town, you might like to arrange a visit to the zoo first, and follow it with a party at home. Another option is to check with the zoo to see if they have facilities for small functions, and take a picnic party along. Alternatively, you could have your own special Zoo Party in the garden, as outlined here.

Invite guests to come dressed as their favourite animal. A costume doesn't have to be elaborate. A paper face mask or snout, a pinned-on tail, and ears made of cardboard and hat elastic will do the trick very well.

**Age group:** four to seven
**Venue:** zoo, or your garden
**Number of guests:** up to 10

### Invitations
Make cards shaped like elephants or your child's favourite animal. Invite guests to dress as an animal and to bring their favourite stuffed animal toys to the party too.

*Clockwise from left: Birds' Nests with Sweet and Sour Sauce, Moo Juice Shakes, Elephant Ears, Growling Gorilla Tamers, Animal Shapes, Cats' Faces and Three Blind Mice.*

*Cat Faces*

swap places and the game continues.

Another game is *No paws allowed*. Put a whole apple onto a paper saucer, one for each guest. Place the saucers on the floor. When all the children are kneeling at a saucer, with hands clasped behind their backs, give a starting signal. They have to eat the apples without using their hands at all. The first to finish is the winner.

**Prizes and Party Favours**
Animal biscuits wrapped in cellophane, animal-shaped rubbers, plastic zoo animals (buy a bag and split it, wrapping each individually).

## CAT FACES

*Preparation time:* 40 minutes
*Cooking time:* 15 minutes
*Makes 24*
*Medium*

½ cup golden syrup
⅓ cup brown sugar
60 g butter
2¼ cups plain flour
2 teaspoons mixed spice
beaten egg, to glaze
1 quantity buttercream frosting (see page 96)
Smarties and licorice for decoration

1. Preheat oven to 180°C and lightly grease oven trays. Combine golden syrup, brown sugar and butter in a pan. Stir over low heat until melted and smooth. Cool to room temperature.
2. Sift flour and spice together into a large bowl. Add cooled syrup mixture and stir well to combine.
3. Roll out half the dough on a lightly floured surface to 2 mm thickness. Cut into 5 cm rounds and place on prepared trays. Roll out remaining dough and cut into long triangles for cats' 'ears'. Brush a little beaten egg onto ears and attach to top of pastry rounds. Bake for 10 minutes until browned. Cool 2–3 minutes on trays before lifting onto wire racks to cool.
4. Spread face of biscuits with frosting and leave ears plain. Decorate with Smarties for eyes and mouth. Cut licorice into 6 thin strips and arrange 3 strips either side of mouth for whiskers.

### Decorations
Collect as many stuffed animal toys as you can from friends and neighbours to add to your own child's collection. Place these in appropriate groups around the garden — all the bears together, the wombats together, and so on. Make zoo signs for each collection — Elephant Enclosure, Reptile House or Platypus Pool — and hang these up. Make enclosures for the groups out of twisted chains of coloured crêpe paper, tied on sticks. Decorate a table of nibbles with a crêpe paper frill, and hang a ZOO KIOSK sign over it. Use paper plates or cups decorated with jungle greenery or animals, or use brightly coloured plastic tableware.

### Food
The menu offers Growling Gorilla Tamers, Moo Juice Shakes, Birds' Nests with Sweet and Sour Sauce, Three Blind Mice, Animal Shapes, Elephant Ears, and Cat Faces.

**Cake:** serve a Piggy Cake.

### Games
Play *The farmer in the dell*, *What's the time, Mr Wolf?*, *Bat the balloon*, and *Wobbling bunnies*. Have a *Blow the balloon* race. Play *Balloon dress-ups*, and have a sack race.

Play *Paddy's black pig* for a good laugh.

Or play *Animalia*. Blindfold six children. Let the others watch. Line up the blindfolded children in a row, not using their names, so that they do not know who their neighbours are. Taking each in turn, and identifying her by touch only, give her an animal; snake, lion and so on. Let each child practise the sound of their animal; hissing, grunting or roaring. Then get them to move out of line and turn around a few times, until the line is thoroughly muddled.

They then have to remake the row in its original order, by listening to the sounds made by each other and placing themselves in the right relative position. Remaining children watch to see if the order is correctly achieved. Observers and players then

## ANIMAL SHAPES

*Preparation time:* 25 minutes
*Cooking time:* 20 minutes
*Makes 18*
*Easy*

4 sheets ready-rolled shortcrust pastry
125 g tasty cheese, grated
125 g cream cheese, softened
¼ cup sour cream
2 tablespoons chopped fresh parsley
1 egg yolk
sesame seeds

1.  Preheat oven to 190°C and lightly grease a flat oven tray. Place two sheets of pastry on a lightly floured surface. In a bowl combine cheeses, cream, parsley and egg white.
2.  Divide cheese mixture between pastry sheets and spread over each sheet. Top with remaining pastry. Roll out pastry lightly so that the layers join together. Using animal shaped cutters, cut pastry into a variety of shapes. Brush surface with beaten egg yolk and sprinkle with sesame seeds.
3.  Bake in oven for 15–20 minutes until pastries are lightly puffed and golden. These are best served warm, though they are still tasty at room temperature.

*Animal Shapes*

## BIRDS' NESTS WITH SWEET AND SOUR SAUCE

*Preparation time:* 40 minutes
*Cooking time:* 25 minutes
*Serves 10*
*Easy*

10 chicken wings
1 egg white
¼ cup cornflour
1 teaspoon soy sauce
90 g rice vermicelli noodles
oil for deep-frying

SAUCE
¼ cup white vinegar
¼ cup white sugar
¼ cup tomato sauce
¼ cup water
1 tablespoon cornflour

1.  Remove wing tip and discard. Cut wing through the joint into two sections. Push chicken flesh to one end of the bone, using a sharp knife to cut through tendons and pry the flesh away from the bone.
2.  Place chicken in a large bowl, with egg white, cornflour and soy sauce. Mix with hands, turning and coating chicken until no flour lumps remain.
3.  Heat oil until very hot. Add a few strands of noodles to test oil temperature. Noodles should puff almost immediately (if they don't, discard them and heat oil further). Cook noodles, half at a time. As soon as noodles puff, lift out with a wire strainer and drain on absorbent paper. Lift chicken wings out of mixture one at a time, and drop into hot oil. Fry about six at a time for 3–5 minutes until chicken is golden and cooked through.
4.  To prepare sauce: blend together all ingredients in a small pan until smooth. Bring to the boil, stirring over medium heat and boil for 1 minute.
5.  To serve: arrange chicken wings on top of noodles on a large serving plate and drizzle a little sauce over the chicken. Serve remaining sauce separately.

*Birds' Nests with Sweet and Sour Sauce*

2. Remove stones from prunes and replace with almonds. Pipe frosting into cavity with almonds. Cut licorice strap into fine short strips and attach with a little frosting to represent whiskers. Attach a larger piece for the tail and pieces of cherry or muskstick for eyes.

3. Chop jelly into cubes and spoon onto a flat white plate. Arrange 'mice' on top of jelly and chill until ready to serve.

## MOO JUICE SHAKES

*Preparation time:* 5 minutes
*Cooking time:* nil
*Serves 6*
*Easy*

400 g fruit-flavoured yoghurt
2 tablespoons honey
1 teaspoon vanilla essence
2 ripe bananas or ¼ peeled seeded
   rockmelon
2 cups chilled milk
4 scoops vanilla ice-cream
grated nutmeg

1. Place all ingredients except nutmeg in a blender bowl. Cover and blend at high speed for 3 minutes.
2. Pour into six glasses and sprinkle with a little grated nutmeg. Serve immediately.

*Growling Gorilla Tamers*

*Moo Juice Shakes*

## GROWLING GORILLA TAMERS

*Preparation time:* 15 minutes
*Cooking time:* 15 minutes
*Serves 10*
*Easy*

10 bananas
200 g chocolate chips
foil for wrapping

1. Preheat oven to 180°C. Peel bananas leaving skin and banana joined at base. Stud banana liberally all over with chocolate chips. Bring up skin to surround banana and wrap tightly in foil.
2. Bake bananas for 10–15 minutes. Remove foil and serve warm. Banana will be lightly cooked and chocolate will be melted throughout.

## THREE BLIND MICE

*Preparation time:* 30 minutes plus chilling time
*Cooking time:* nil
*Serves 20*
*Easy*

1 x 85 g packet yellow jelly
20 prunes
20 almonds
½ quantity vanilla flavoured buttercream frosting (see recipe page 96)
1 licorice strap
red cherries or musksticks

1. Make jelly according to instructions on packet using only 1½ cups water. Chill until jelly is set firmly.

*Three Blind Mice*

## ELEPHANT EARS

*Preparation time:* 15 minutes
*Cooking time:* 10 minutes
*Makes 15*
*Easy*

oil for deep-frying
1 x 125g packet poppadums
poppy seeds

1.  Heat oil until surface appears to be moving and oil is hot. Drop in one poppadum to test it. Poppadum should expand and puff almost immediately. If it does not, allow oil to get hotter.
2.  Cook poppadums in hot oil a few at a time, lift out of oil and whilst still hot sprinkle with poppy seeds. Drain on absorbent paper.

*Piggy Cake*

## PIGGY CAKE

*Preparation time:* 1 hour
*Cooking time:* 50 minutes
*Easy*

2 x 350 g packets cake mix or
   2 quantities butter cake batter
   (see page 96)
1 quantity butter icing
   (see page 96)
few drops pink food colouring
1 licorice strap
Smarties
2 cups coconut
green food colouring

1.  Preheat oven to 180°C. Grease and line both a 20 cm round and a 20 cm square cake tin. Make the cakes according to directions on the packet or following recipe. Divide mixture evenly between prepared tins and bake for 40–50 minutes or until cooked. Leave cake to cool in tin before turning out. Trim the cakes so they are both the same height.
2.  From the square cake, cut a 10 cm round for the snout and two ears (see diagram 1). Colour butter icing pale pink. Use two-thirds to cover the round cake and the ears. Colour remaining one-third of the icing a darker shade of pink and use this to cover the snout.
3.  Place the cake on a covered cake board, positioning snout and ears appropriately (see diagram 2). Use Smarties for eyes and nostrils. Cut the licorice strap to form whiskers, ears and eyelashes. Colour the coconut green, sprinkle around the head and decorate with Smarties and any remaining licorice strips.

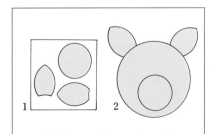

1.  Placement diagram for cutting snout and ears.
2.  Assemble the iced cake pieces on a board.

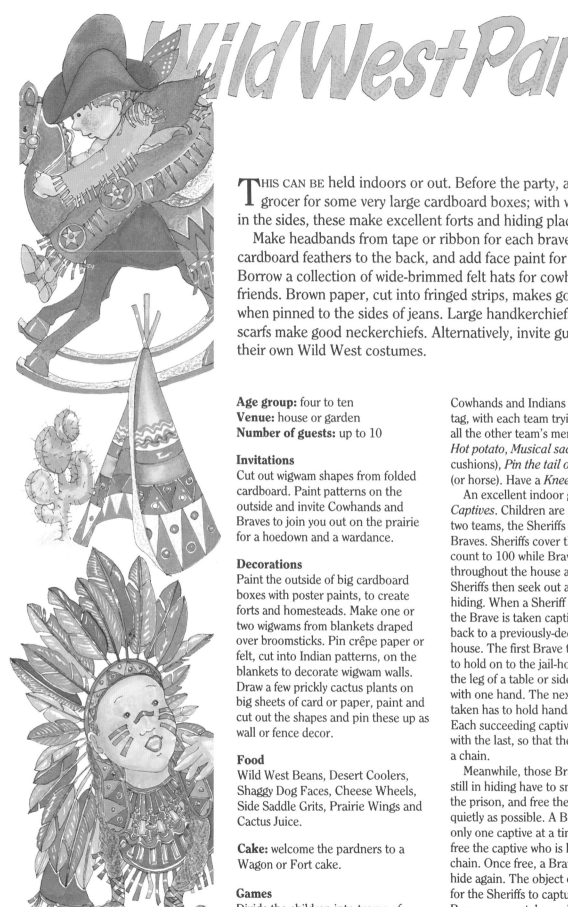

# Wild West Party

THIS CAN BE held indoors or out. Before the party, ask your local grocer for some very large cardboard boxes; with windows cut in the sides, these make excellent forts and hiding places.

Make headbands from tape or ribbon for each brave. Add cardboard feathers to the back, and add face paint for extra fun. Borrow a collection of wide-brimmed felt hats for cowhands from friends. Brown paper, cut into fringed strips, makes good chaps when pinned to the sides of jeans. Large handkerchiefs or square scarfs make good neckerchiefs. Alternatively, invite guests to create their own Wild West costumes.

**Age group:** four to ten
**Venue:** house or garden
**Number of guests:** up to 10

### Invitations
Cut out wigwam shapes from folded cardboard. Paint patterns on the outside and invite Cowhands and Braves to join you out on the prairie for a hoedown and a wardance.

### Decorations
Paint the outside of big cardboard boxes with poster paints, to create forts and homesteads. Make one or two wigwams from blankets draped over broomsticks. Pin crêpe paper or felt, cut into Indian patterns, on the blankets to decorate wigwam walls. Draw a few prickly cactus plants on big sheets of card or paper, paint and cut out the shapes and pin these up as wall or fence decor.

### Food
Wild West Beans, Desert Coolers, Shaggy Dog Faces, Cheese Wheels, Side Saddle Grits, Prairie Wings and Cactus Juice.

**Cake:** welcome the pardners to a Wagon or Fort cake.

### Games
Divide the children into teams of Cowhands and Indians for a game of tag, with each team trying to round up all the other team's members. Play *Hot potato*, *Musical saddles* (or cushions), *Pin the tail on the donkey* (or horse). Have a *Knee balloon race*.

An excellent indoor game is *Captives*. Children are divided into two teams, the Sheriffs and the Braves. Sheriffs cover their eyes and count to 100 while Braves scatter throughout the house and hide. The Sheriffs then seek out all those in hiding. When a Sheriff finds a Brave, the Brave is taken captive and taken back to a previously-decided jail-house. The first Brave taken there has to hold on to the jail-house bars — the leg of a table or side of a chair — with one hand. The next captive taken has to hold hands with the first. Each succeeding captive links hands with the last, so that the captives form a chain.

Meanwhile, those Braves who are still in hiding have to sneak back to the prison, and free the captives as quietly as possible. A Brave may free only one captive at a time, and must free the captive who is last in the chain. Once free, a Brave goes off to hide again. The object of the game — for the Sheriffs to capture all the Braves — may take a while to achieve!

**Prizes and Party Favours**
Small plastic Wild West toy figures
(buy a bag from a department store
and split it up); silver nuggets (pieces
of fudge or cookies wrapped in silver
foil) and water pistols.

*Clockwise from left: Desert Coolers, Wild
West Beans, Side Saddle Grits, Cactus Juice,
Prairie Wings, Shaggy Dog Faces, and
Cheese Wheels (centre)*

## SIDE SADDLE GRITS

*Preparation time:* 10 minutes
*Cooking time:* 10 minutes
*Serves 10*
*Easy*

5 cobs corn
1 tablespoon sugar
125 g butter
thick toothpicks (older children only)

1.  Peel away green covering from
cobs of corn and remove 'silk'. Break
cobs in half. Place corn into a large
pan of cold water, add sugar and a few
outer leaves of the corn. Bring to boil
and cook 8–10 minutes until corn is
tender.
2.  Drain corn and toss in butter.
Insert a toothpick in each end of the
corn to serve.

*Shaggy Dog Faces*

*Wild West Beans*

## SHAGGY DOG FACES

*Preparation time:* 20 minutes
*Cooking time:* 2 minutes
*Makes 18*
*Easy*

4 cups Rice Crispies
1½ cups icing sugar, sifted
1 cup desiccated coconut
3 tablespoons cocoa
250 g vegetable fat
a little frosting or icing
shredded coconut
jelly beans
red glacé cherries
white or pink marshmallows

1. In a bowl combine Rice Crispies with icing sugar, coconut and cocoa. Melt vegetable fat over gentle heat, cool slightly and pour over dry ingredients. Stir to mix thoroughly.
2. Divide evenly between paper cake cases. Chill in the refrigerator to set.
3. Attach decorations with a little icing — coconut for hair, pieces of jelly beans for eyes, a glacé cherry for mouth and a marshmallow for a hat.

## WILD WEST BEANS

*Preparation time:* 15 minutes
*Cooking time:* 15 minutes
*Serves 10*
*Easy*

200 g corn chips
1 x 440 g can baked beans
150 g ham, cut into 1 cm pieces
200 g grated processed cheddar cheese

*Cactus Juice*

1. Preheat oven to 180°C. Spread a layer of corn chips on a large flat platter. Spoon over a quarter of the baked beans, sprinkle with a quarter of the ham and cheese. Top with corn chips and repeat layers until all ingredients are used. Finish with a light sprinkling of cheese.
2. Heat through in the oven for 10–15 minutes until cheese melts. Serve hot with a few extra corn chips if desired.

## CACTUS JUICE

*Preparation time:* 10 minutes plus chilling time
*Cooking time:* nil
*Serves 10*
*Easy*

2 litres apple juice
2 tablespoons honey
½ cucumber, seeded and finely sliced
1 x 750 ml bottle lemonade, chilled
1 x 750 ml bottle soda water, chilled
ice-cubes
fresh mint leaves for garnish

1. Mix together apple juice, honey and cucumber. Pour into a large serving jug or bowl and chill thoroughly.
2. To serve: add lemonade, soda, and ice-cubes. Float a few mint leaves as a garnish.

## DESERT COOLERS

*Preparation time:* 30 minutes plus
   freezing time
*Cooking time:* nil
*Makes 12*
*Easy*

1 fresh pineapple
500 ml plain yoghurt
1 x 85 g packet lemon flavoured
   jelly
2 cups shredded coconut

1.  Peel pineapple and remove any brown spots and eyes. Cut pineapple in half, and remove core. Cut each half in three wedges, and cut wedges in half horizontally. This will give 12 small wedges in all. Insert a lollipop stick into each wedge. Place in freezer until partially frozen.
2.  Mix together yoghurt and jelly crystals and stir briskly over a bowl of warm water until yoghurt has thinned and crystals are beginning to dissolve.
3.  Dip each wedge of pineapple into yoghurt mixture then dip into coconut. Stand sticks in a piece of polystyrene or chunks of vegetables, and return to freezer until frozen.

*Desert Coolers*

*Cheese Wheels*

## CHEESE WHEELS

*Preparation time:* 20 minutes
*Cooking time:* nil
*Serves 8*
*Easy*

250 g processed or mild cheddar, sliced
   into 1cm slices
chunks of cabana, gherkins and dried
   apricots
toothpicks

1.  Using a round scone cutter, cut cheese slices into discs.
2.  Thread 2 cheese discs onto each toothpick, alternating with a cabana, gherkins and apricots. For younger children, omit toothpicks and pile onto biscuits.

HINT
Cabana is a continental salami style sausage similar to cabanossi. It is available at large supermarkets and delicatessens. Whole cherry tomatoes can be used instead of apricots.

*Wagon Cake*

## WAGON CAKE

*Preparation time:* 1¼ hours
*Cooking time:* 40 minutes
*Easy*

2 x 350 g packets cake mix or
   2 quantities butter cake batter
   (see page 96)
3–4 tablespoons cocoa
hot water
1 quantity basic butter icing
   (see page 96)
red food colouring
yellow food colouring
12 round chocolate biscuits
2 licorice strips
chocolate chips

1.  Preheat oven to 180°C. Grease
both a 14 x 8 cm cylindrical loaf tin
and a 14 x 8 cm loaf tin. Make the
cakes according to directions on the
packet or following recipe. Divide
mixture between prepared tins and
bake for 35–40 minutes or until
cooked. Cool. Cakes may need to be
trimmed to equal length.
2.  Dissolve cocoa in hot water. When
cool beat into half the butter icing.
Divide the remaining portion in half
again, colouring one yellow and one
red.
3.  Make two piles of four round
chocolate biscuits, joining the biscuits
together with a little butter icing.
Cover the rectangular cake with
chocolate butter icing and smooth
with a knife, to form the base of the
wagon. Place the two piles of
chocolate biscuits on a plate to act as
a support for the cake and position
the wagon base on these. To make
the top of the wagon, cover the
cylindrical cake in strips of red and
yellow icing. Smooth with a knife.
Place the top onto the wagon base

## PRAIRIE WINGS

*Preparation time:* 50 minutes
*Cooking time:* 10 minutes
*Makes 24*
*Medium*

12 chicken wings
1 cup plain flour
½ teaspoon garlic powder
½ teaspoon cinnamon
½ teaspoon black pepper
½ teaspoon dried oregano
½ teaspoon dried parsley flakes
pinch paprika
oil for deep-frying

1.  Cut chicken wings into three
pieces, cutting through joints. Discard
wing tips. Using a sharp knife cut
flesh around the top of each joint
through to the bone. Push flesh
down, prying it away from the bone
until it is all pushed to one end but
still intact.
2.  Mix together flour, herbs and

spices in a large plastic bag. Add
chicken and shake bag to coat
chicken with flour.
3.  Remove chicken from flour and
deep-fry in hot oil for 3–5 minutes
until crisp, golden and cooked
through. Drain on absorbent paper
and serve hot.

*Prairie Wings*

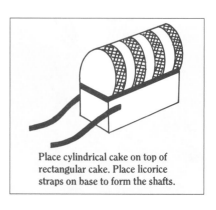

Place cylindrical cake on top of
rectangular cake. Place licorice
straps on base to form the shafts.

and join with icing.

4. Cut strips of licorice to cover the join of the two cakes. Cut two more strips to form the shafts. Attach these to the sides (see diagram). Pipe the child's name along the side of the wagon in white butter icing, using a piping bag. Pipe spokes on the remaining four chocolate biscuits to form wheels. Attach these to each corner of the wagon, using icing. Sprinkle chocolate chips over the plate to represent the ground.

## FORT CAKE

*Preparation time:* 1½ hours
*Cooking time:* 45 minutes
*Easy*

1 x 350 g packet cake mix or
   1 quantity butter cake batter
   (see page 96)

ICING
½ quantity butter icing (see page 96)
1½ tablespoons cocoa
1 tablespoon hot water
½ cup icing sugar
water
2 x 200 g packets chocolate finger
   biscuits
Wild West figures

1. Preheat oven to 180°C. Grease and line a 20 cm square cake tin. Make the cake according to directions on the packet or following recipe. Turn into prepared tin and bake for 40–45 minutes or until cooked. Cool before turning out.
2. To prepare icing: dissolve cocoa in hot water to form a thick paste. Add to butter icing, and beat well to blend. Coat cake with icing and place on a cake board.
3. Prepare plain icing by mixing icing sugar and a little water to a piping consistency. Pipe 'Happy Birthday' and the birthday child's name onto the cake.
4. Cut about 1 cm off the ends of eight biscuits and place these at intervals around the cake, cut ends down (see diagram 1). Use the remaining biscuits to surround cake completely to give a fort effect (see diagram 2). Place Wild West figures at appropriate places on cake and on the board outside the fort.

*Fort Cake*

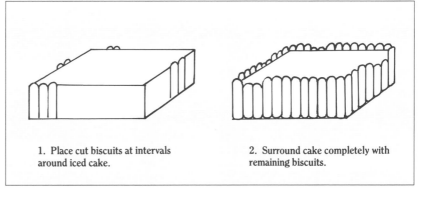

1. Place cut biscuits at intervals around iced cake.

2. Surround cake completely with remaining biscuits.

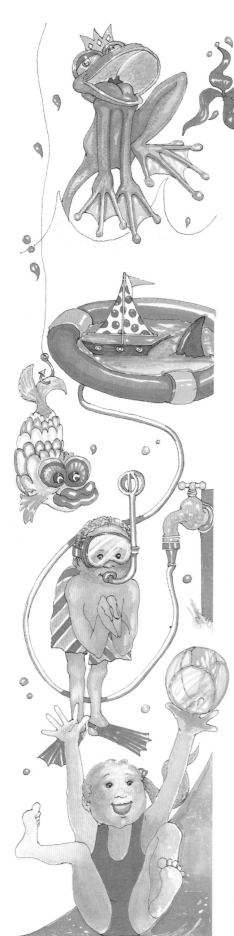

# Water Party

T HIS IS TERRIFIC for younger children, and sometimes tempts the older mavericks too. Best held in summer, it can also be very successful in a mild autumn or hot spring season. While the children enjoy splashing, your garden benefits as well.

It's wise to check with the local council in very hot weather, to see if water restrictions are currently in force.

You don't need a pool for a water party — the basic equipment is a hose, a sprinkler, and one or two sheets of plastic (inexpensive sheets are obtainable from most hardware stores or gardening outlets). It helps to have neighbours who won't mind a bit of noise for a couple of hours.

Dress requirements are simple: guests wear swimming costumes and bring a towel. It is a good idea to ask them to bring a change of clothes, so that if they get too chilly, they can change and warm up.

**Age group:** four to eight
**Venue:** the garden
**Number of guests:** 10–12

### Invitations
Cut out a fish shape from folded card. Borrow your child's wax crayons and draw scales and features in white or yellow wax, then paint over the wax with blue watercolour — you'll get a glistening wet fish effect. As well as giving the details of the party, add a note about the theme, for example, 'This is a water party. B.Y.O. towels, wear a swimming costume, and let's make a splash!'

### Decorations
Cut out paper fish and boat shapes from coloured card and hang them from trees and shrubs. Cut blue and green crêpe paper into wavy narrow strips, and hang the streamers from the washline or eaves to make fronds of seaweed. Pinch or pull the edges of the crêpe for a wavy effect. Paper plates, cups and napkins featuring fish are available from most stores.

### Food
Fish 'n Chips, Pizza Subs, Rainbow Pond, Tropical Fish on sticks, Frankfurter Sailboats, Shark-infested Waters, Life Savers.

**Cake:** Tiny the Tugboat will add a nautical touch.

### Games
Spread a sheet of plastic on the lawn and turn the hose on lightly, so that a steady trickle of water runs across the sheet. This makes an invitingly slippery surface and becomes a water slide, whether on the level or on a slight slope.

Alternatively, hand out three big

balloons. Have the children stand in a circle around the sprinkler, with the sprinkler turned up high. Children must throw the balloons across the water fountain, to the child opposite. With three balloons being thrown simultaneously, and often being deflected by the sprinkler, this game leads to a giggling tumble of children scrambling to catch errant balloons.

Play *Jump the broom*, substituting the sprinkler for the broom.

Bring out a bowl of soapy water and have a bubble-blowing competition. Bubbles can be blown through plastic pipes, twists of plastic-coated wire, or through the 'O' formed by a forefinger tip touching the thumb.

Play *Sardines*, *On the bank*, *In the river*, or *Froggy, froggy, may we cross your shining river?* Have a *Fishing competition* or a *Water race*.

**Prizes and Party Favours**
Marshmallow fish or frogs from the local sweet store; small plastic water toys such as boats or ducks, or ping-pong balls. Water pistols.

*Clockwise from left: Pizza Subs, Shark Infested Waters, Rainbow Pond, Frankfurter Sailboats. Tropical Fish on Sticks, Fish 'n Chips, Lifesavers, The Big Wheel.*

*Rainbow Pond*

## FISH 'N CHIPS

*Preparation time:* 45 minutes
*Cooking time:* 30 minutes
*Serves 10*
*Medium*

750 g white fish fillets
1 egg, lightly beaten
¼ cup milk
1 cup plain flour
2 cups dried breadcrumbs
8 potatoes
oil for deep-frying
lemon wedges or vinegar for serving

1.  Cut fish into 3cm pieces, removing any bones. Beat together egg and milk. Coat fish in flour, dip in egg mixture, then into breadcrumbs. Press crumbs on firmly. Chill until ready to cook.
2.  Peel potatoes. Cut potato lengthways into 1cm wide finger lengths. Rinse under cold water and pat dry in a tea-towel or kitchen paper. Heat oil in a deep fryer, lower half the chips into the oil and cook for 5 minutes. Lift out and drain on absorbent paper. Reheat oil and repeat process with remaining chips.
3.  When ready to serve: reheat oil and cook chips until crisp and golden. Drain on absorbent paper and keep warm in the oven. Cook fish, a few pieces at a time, for 1–2 minutes until golden and cooked through. Drain on absorbent paper and keep warm. Serve hot with a little vinegar or lemon wedges.

*If fish pieces take longer to cook than 2 minutes, the oil isn't hot enough — increase the temperature to ensure fish cooks on the inside without burning on the outside.

*Fish 'n Chips*

## RAINBOW POND

*Preparation time:* 35 minutes plus chilling time
*Cooking time:* 2 minutes
*Serves 10*
*Easy*

4½ cups apple juice
1 x 85 g packet orange-flavoured jelly
1 x 85 g packet lime-flavoured jelly
1 x 85 g packet strawberry-flavoured jelly
1 x 425 g can apricot halves, well drained
½ ripe honeydew melon, with the flesh shaped into balls by a melon baller
1 x 250 g punnet strawberries, hulled and halved
yoghurt, cream or ice cream for serving

1.  Make up different jelly flavours separately using apple juice instead of water. Allow to cool until mixture thickens slightly.
2.  To assemble: into a clear glass 2 litre serving bowl pour thickened orange jelly mixture and apricot halves. Refrigerate until set.
3.  Gently spoon lime jelly and melon balls on top of apricot layer. Refrigerate until set.
4.  Spoon on strawberry jelly and strawberry halves as a final layer. Chill for several hours until firmly set.
5.  When jelly is set, serve accompanied by ice-cream, freshly whipped cream or plain yoghurt.

28

## LIFE SAVERS

*Preparation time:* 25 minutes
*Cooking time:* 1 hour
*Makes 10*
*Medium*

2 egg whites
½ cup caster sugar
300 ml thickened cream
raspberry jam for spreading
fine red ribbon

1. Preheat oven to 150°C. Grease an oven tray and sprinkle liberally with cornflour, or line tray with baking paper. Mark 5 cm circles on it.
2. Beat egg whites into stiff peaks. Add sugar, a tablespoon at a time, beating well between each addition.
3. Fill a piping bag and pipe around edge of circles on tray. Bake for 20–30 minutes or until meringue is dry. Turn oven off, letting meringues dry in cooling oven.
4. Near serving time, join meringues together in pairs with jam and cream. Thread ribbon through centre and around rings, lifebuoy-style. (If filled too far in advance, meringues become moist and soft.)

*Life Savers*

*Shark-infested Waters*

## SHARK-INFESTED WATERS

*Preparation time:* 5 minutes
*Cooking time:* nil
*Serves 8*
*Easy*

1 x 850 ml can pineapple juice
1 cup orange juice
½ cup lime juice cordial
3 passionfruit
1 x 285 ml bottle dry ginger ale
2 x 285 ml bottles lemonade, chilled
1 orange, cut into segments
2 slices pineapple, cut into 1cm chunks
ice-cubes

1. In a large jug or bowl, mix together juices, cordial and passionfruit. Chill thoroughly.
2. Stir in ginger ale and lemonade. Add orange and pineapple together with a few ice-cubes.

*Frankfurter Sailboats*

*The Big Wheel*

## FRANKFURTER SAILBOATS

*Preparation time:* 15 minutes
*Cooking time:* 5 minutes
*Makes 8*
*Easy*

8 frankfurters
8 long bread rolls
soft butter
8 short bamboo skewers
4 single cheese slices, halved diagonally
8 cherry tomatoes
tomato sauce, mustard and gherkin relish, as desired
celery, carrot and zucchini sticks for serving

1. Place frankfurters in a pan, cover with cold water and slowly heat until boiling. Drain.
2. Split rolls and spread lightly with butter, if desired. Place a frankfurter in each roll.
3. Insert a skewer into each cheese slice, then through a tomato. Stand skewers upright through one end of each frankfurter with cheese at the top to make sails. Serve with condiments and vegetable sticks.

## TROPICAL FISH ON STICKS

*Preparation time:* 15 minutes plus chilling and freezing time
*Cooking time:* 2 minutes
*Serves 10*
*Easy*

3 oranges
1 x 85 g packet orange-flavoured jelly
½ cup orange juice

1. Peel oranges leaving outer white pith intact. Break oranges into segments, arrange them on a flat tray and place in the freezer until frozen.
2. Make jelly with orange juice instead of water. Cool in the refrigerator until jelly begins to thicken.
3. Skewer orange segments with toothpicks. Dip each segment into jelly, allowing drips to fall back into bowl. Stand each toothpick in a piece of polystyrene or a potato and place in the freezer to set. For younger children, remove toothpicks before serving. Serve frozen.

## THE BIG WHEEL

*Preparation time:* 30 minutes
*Cooking time:* 20 minutes
*Makes 1 cake with 12 sections*
*Medium*

2 cups self-raising flour
30 g butter cut into small pieces
⅓ cup caster sugar
¼ cup sultanas
1 egg, beaten
150 ml milk
½ cup strawberry jam or other jam, warmed
6 musksticks or thick licorice twists

1. Preheat oven to 220°C and grease a 20 cm ring tin with melted butter. Sift flour into a large bowl. Rub in butter lightly, using fingertips.
2. Mix in sugar and sultanas. Combine egg and milk. Make a well in the centre of the flour. Pour in liquid all at once, reserving about a teaspoon for glazing. Mix quickly into a soft dough.
3. Turn onto a floured board (use self-raising flour). Knead lightly. Roll out to form a rectangle about 1.5 cm thick. Spread jam over dough. Roll up as a swiss roll and cut into 2 cm lengths. Place in prepared tin cut side up. Glaze with milk. Bake for 15–20 minutes or until golden brown. Mixture should be just leaving the sides of the tin. Cool on wire rack. Insert musksticks or licorice, as spokes on the wheel. Serve sliced and spread with butter.

*Pizza Subs*

1. Preheat oven to 180°C and grease two 18 x 28 cm shallow tins. Make cakes according to directions on the packet or following recipe. Pour into prepared tins and bake for 35 minutes or until cooked. Cool.
2. Cut base of boat out of first cake (see diagram 1). Cut second cake into 3 pieces for top decks (see diagram 2).
3. Tint one-third of prepared buttercream frosting bright blue and cover first tier. Cover the remaining three pieces with untinted frosting, then assemble as shown in the photograph.
4. Make portholes from round candies. Cut snakes lengthways into strips and use them to make deck trim. Press marshmallows and candle in place, and finish with a small anchor.

## PIZZA SUBS

*Preparation time:* 20 minutes
*Cooking time:* 15 minutes
*Makes 12*
*Easy*

6 long bread rolls
250 g butter, melted
1 cup tomato purée
1 tablespoon tomato paste
1 teaspoon dried oregano
pinch dried basil
pinch sugar
500 g mozzarella cheese, finely grated
1 green capsicum, halved, seeded and
   finely sliced
1 red capsicum, halved, seeded and
   finely sliced
250 g ham, cut into 1 cm pieces
1 x 225 g can pineapple pieces, drained

1. Preheat oven to 200°C. Split rolls in half lengthways. Brush cut surface and outside crust with melted butter.
2. Combine tomato purée, tomato paste, herbs and sugar. Spread over cut surface of bread. Top with grated cheese and arrange capsicum, ham and pineapple over surface.
3. Bake for 10–15 minutes or until cheese melts and browns. Serve hot.

## TINY THE TUGBOAT

*Preparation time:* 50 minutes
*Cooking time:* 35 minutes
*Easy*

2 x 350 g packets cake mix or
   2 quantities butter cake batter
   (see page 96)
2 quantities buttercream frosting
   (see page 96)
blue food colouring
red and white round candies
red snake jujubes
white marshmallows
candle
a small toy anchor

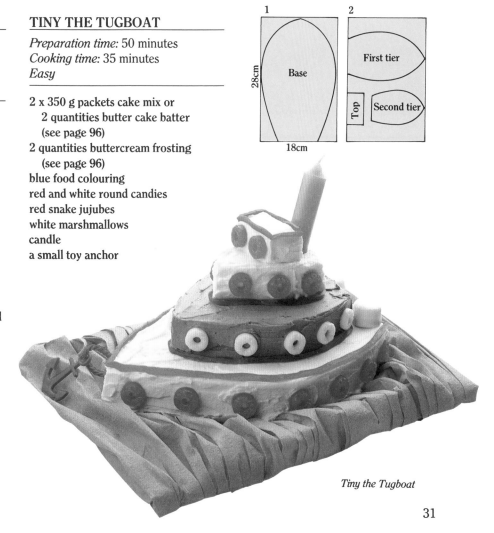

*Tiny the Tugboat*

31

# Pirate Party

T HIS THEME is enormously popular with children aged from five to nine. Providing a costume at the door as each guest arrives takes very little preparation beforehand, and gets the party going quickly. Make each guest an eyepatch from a triangle of black cardboard and a piece of hat elastic. Make gold earrings from brass curtain rings with a loop of cotton attached, to loop over the ears. If you have an old curtain or table cloth that's due for the ragbag, tear it into triangles or strips, and have each child tie the strips around their heads to add to the piratical look. You could make more elaborate additions: cardboard swords for each guest, and cummerbunds.

**Age group:** five to nine
**Venue:** house or garden
**Number of guests:** up to 12

### Invitations
Folded card, cut to the shape of a treasure chest and suitably illustrated by the host, could be opened to invite fellow brigands aboard the *Good Ship Tamsin Martin* (use your child's name). If you are providing eye patches and scarves, ask guests to wear jeans. Alternatively, ask them to dress as pirates.

### Decorations
Paint parrots, treasure chests, and palm trees on large sheets of card or butcher's paper. Cut these out and pin them up. As a highlight, draw a sailing ship with a Jolly Roger flying from the topmost mast. Hang other flags from the ceiling or from trees. Add cardboard cut-out sharks and a mermaid or two. A washing basket filled with balloons makes a good treasure chest; even the most blood-thirsty pirate enjoys balloons.

If the party is held in the evening, pirates' lamps add to the atmosphere and are easy to make. For each, you need a paper packet, sand, water, a glass jar and a candle. Half-fill the packet with sand. In the sand, stand

a glass jar which is one-quarter full of water. Stand the candle in the water. When the candle is lit, the paper packet will glow with a soft light. (Should the lamp be knocked over accidentally, the sand and water will dowse the flame quickly.)

### Food
Calculated to make the hungriest pirate's mouth water — Wooden Legs, Pirate Ships, Banana Planks, Cannon Balls, Deadly Decks and Poison Potion.

**Cake:** Long John Silver's Treasure Chest.

### Games
Have a hat-making session early in the party, so that each child makes a

triangular pirate's hat for her- or himself. Make these from sheets of newspaper, or from butcher's paper cut to the same size as newspaper.

Use tapes of traditional sea shanties for musical accompaniment to play *Musical hats*, *Musical sets*, or *Jump the shark* (otherwise known as *Jump the broom*). Play *Pass the oranges*; have a *Balloon fight*, or a *Knee balloon race*. Arrange a treasure hunt

and a three-legged race. Have a *Back-to-back race*.

Make steps out of chairs, and have the steps lead up to a tabletop covered with brown paper. Place a pile of soft cushions, or a mattress, on the floor at the far side of the table. As a forfeit, or for children who go out during other games, let them walk the plank by climbing onto the table and jumping off into the cushions.

Play *The Captain's coming*. Nominate one side of the room to be port, and another to be starboard. Also nominate places or pieces of furniture to be a rowboat, the anchor, the main mast, the cannon etc. All children group in the centre of the

*Clockwise from left: Wooden Legs, Banana Planks, Deadly Decks, Poison Potion, Cannon Balls and Pirate Ships.*

30 minutes or until chicken is cooked through, turning and basting chicken every 10 minutes. Chicken is cooked when juices run clear if pierced through the thickest section of the leg.

3. Tie 2 pretzels to the base of each leg with a long chive, to represent Long John Silver's crutch. Serve hot or cold.

*Wooden Legs*

## POISON POTION

*Preparation time:* 30 minutes plus
    overnight standing time
*Cooking time:* 5 minutes
*Makes 10 cups*
*Easy*

6¼ cups boiling water
5 cups sugar
2 lemons, juiced and rind finely grated
2 large oranges, juiced and rind finely grated
30 g citric acid
15 g tartaric acid
15 g Epsom salts

1. Pour boiling water over sugar in a pan, then stir over gentle heat until sugar dissolves. Stir in grated rind and strained juice.
2. Stir in remaining ingredients. Cover with a cloth and leave overnight. Pour into sterilised bottles and store in the refrigerator. When ready to serve, dilute with iced water.

*Poison Potion*

room. Call out the key phrase and add a command, for example 'The Captain's coming — run to starboard!' or, 'The Captain's coming — scrub the decks!' The last person to reach starboard or to start scrubbing the decks is out. Other commands could be to salute, to run to the rowboat, to lift the anchor and so on.

Play *Shipwrecked*, a type of tag. Scatter cushions on the floor. Only the catcher (or Shark) may touch the floor. The other children must flee the Shark, moving only from cushion to cushion. Anyone landing in the sea (i.e. on the floor) is shipwrecked, and may be caught by the Shark.

### Prizes and Party Favours
Pieces of eight (chocolate coins covered in gold foil). Popcorn necklaces. Stickers featuring parrots, rainbows or boats. Bars of silver (muesli or chocolate bars wrapped in silver foil).

## WOODEN LEGS

*Preparation time:* 10 minutes
*Cooking time:* 40 minutes
*Serves 10*
*Easy*

10 chicken drumsticks

BASTE
4 tablespoons dark soy sauce
1 tablespoon honey
1 clove garlic, crushed
1 tablespoon tomato sauce
20 pretzels
10 long chives, soaked for 5 minutes in hot water

1. Preheat oven to 200°C. Place drumsticks on a wire rack in a baking dish containing a little water. Roast in the oven for 10 minutes.
2. To prepare baste: combine all remaining ingredients except pretzels and chives and brush the baste over chicken drumsticks. Roast a further

## CANNON BALLS

*Preparation time:* 25 minutes
*Cooking time:* 5 minutes
*Serves 8*
*Easy*

500g sausage meat
½ cup crushed, plain savoury biscuits
¼ cup grated tasty cheese
1 egg, lightly beaten
¼ cup evaporated milk
1 tablespoon fruit chutney
pinch pepper
oil for shallow frying

1.  In a bowl combine all ingredients except oil. Take small portions and form into 2cm balls. Shallow-fry in oil until browned and cooked through. Serve hot on wooden toothpicks.

NOTE
These can be made one or two days ahead and reheated.

## DEADLY DECKS

*Preparation time:* 20 minutes
*Cooking time:* 25 minutes
*Makes 18*
*Medium*

500 g sausage meat
2 tablespoons plain flour
2 tablespoons tomato sauce
1 small onion, grated
1 tablespoon chopped fresh parsley
1 x 350 g packet prepared puff pastry
beaten egg
tomato sauce for serving

1.  Preheat oven to 200°C. In a pan combine sausage meat, flour, sauce, onion and parsley. Stir over low heat for 2–3 minutes, then simmer for another 10 minutes. Turn out onto a plate to cool.
2.  Roll out pastry thinly. Cut into strips 8–10 cm wide. Spoon meat mixture down the centre of each strip, leaving a margin on pastry edges to fold over. Brush edges with milk or water and fold over to seal.
3.  Glaze pastry with a little beaten egg. Cut into 10 cm lengths. Arrange, seam side down, on prepared trays and bake for 15 minutes, or until pastry is brown and crisp. Serve hot with tomato sauce.

*Cannon Balls*

*Deadly Decks*

## PIRATE SHIPS

*Preparation time:* 30 minutes
*Cooking time:* 15 minutes
*Makes 24*
*Medium*

1¾ cups plain flour
90 g butter
1 tablespoon iced water
2 egg yolks
¼ cup barbecue sauce
1 stick cabanossi or other sausage, cut into 1 cm slices
60 g mozzarella cheese, grated
1 onion, finely chopped
4 gherkins, thinly sliced

1.  Preheat oven to 200°C.
2.  Sift flour into a bowl. Rub in butter until mixture resembles coarse breadcrumbs. Mix together iced water and egg yolks. Add to mixture and work through with a flat-bladed knife.
3.  Mould into a ball and knead lightly. Roll out two-thirds of pastry thinly on a floured board. Cut out pastry shapes to fit boat-shaped or tartlet tins, line each hollow or tin with pastry and prick pastry with a fork. Bake for 10 minutes or until pastry is golden.

*Pirate Ships*

*Banana Planks*

## BANANA PLANKS

*Preparation time:* 10 minutes
*Cooking time:* nil
*Serves 10*
*Easy*

5 ripe bananas, peeled and quartered lengthways
5 passionfruit, pulped
5 kiwi fruit, peeled and chopped
¼ small pineapple, peeled, cored and roughly chopped
1 litre vanilla ice-cream
1 cup chocolate flavoured syrup
10 ice-cream wafers

1.  Arrange two banana quarters in each individual sundae dish. Spoon over passionfruit pulp, kiwi fruit and pineapple chunks.
2.  Arrange 2 small scoops of ice-cream over fruit in each dish. Drizzle over a little chocolate sauce and garnish with an ice-cream wafer.

4. Roll out remaining pastry thinly and cut into triangles to form sail shapes. Thread a toothpick through centre of each pastry sail. Lay them flat on a lightly greased oven tray and bake for 5–7 minutes or until golden.

5. Spoon barbecue sauce into the base of each pastry case. Top with gherkin, onion and grated cheese. Place a slice of cabanossi in the centre of each boat and return to the oven for 5 minutes or until cheese melts and browns lightly. Remove from oven and while still hot, insert pastry sail. Serve immediately.

## LONG JOHN SILVER'S TREASURE CHEST

*Preparation time:* 1 hour
*Cooking time:* 45 minutes
*Medium*

2 x 350 g packets cake mix or
   2 quantities butter cake batter
   (see page 96)
1 quantity butter icing (see page 96)
2 tablespoons coffee essence
chocolate sprinkles
5 toothpicks
200 g marzipan
extra coffee essence
licorice
chocolate gold coins
costume jewellery

1. Preheat oven to 180°C and grease two 20 x 8 cm loaf tins. Make the cakes according to directions on packet or following recipe. Turn mixture into prepared tins and bake for 40–45 minutes. Cool.

2. Add coffee essence to the butter icing and ice the top and sides of one of the cakes to form the chest, and the top and sides of the other cake to form the lid. Reserve enough icing for final decoration.

3. Place one cake on a cake board, and sprinkle the top with chocolate sprinkles. This forms the base of the chest. Secure five toothpicks along the back edge of the bottom cake, against which to rest the lid (see diagram 1).

4. Knead the marzipan until pliable. Add enough coffee essence to make marzipan a dark brown and continue to knead to distribute the colour evenly. Roll out and cut two 20 x 3 cm strips. Lay these over the two ends of the lid to look like straps. Using the remaining marzipan, form a handle and a keyhole for the chest. Cut licorice into a keyhole shape and place on the marzipan before securing to the cake.

5. To the remaining butter icing, add extra coffee essence to make the icing a darker brown. Fill a piping bag, and using a plain nozzle pipe around the edges and bottom of the chest, and pipe initials on the lid.

6. Fill the chest with chocolate gold coins and costume jewellery. Secure handle to chest. Place the lid on the cake, resting it against the toothpicks at the rear edge (see diagram 2).

*Long John Silver's Treasure Chest*

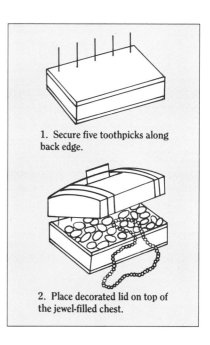

1. Secure five toothpicks along back edge.

2. Place decorated lid on top of the jewel-filled chest.

# Kite Party

THIS ONE IS great for high flyers. It's a party that can be enjoyed by most ages. If it is held for younger children, parents will probably get involved too.

Plan to hold the kite-flying time of the party in the nearest open space — the park or a football field. Have the business part of it (eating and kite-making) at home.

Before the party, check that kites will be clear of power lines in the kite-flying area, and check the safest route for walking to it. On the way there and back, younger children could make a chain by holding onto a length of rope in pairs. All children should be seen safely across busy roads or intersections.

**Age group:** five to eleven
**Venue:** home and an open space, such as the park
**Number of guests:** up to 10

### Invitations
Make cardboard kites small enough to fit into envelopes for posting. Write party details on the kite face. Add a tail made from thread and twists of coloured tissue paper. If the weather is likely to be cool, remind guests to bring jackets to wear outside.

*Clockwise from top left: Swirls and Twists, Kite Cake, Smooth Landings, Clouds, Kite Tails, High Flying Kites, Reels of String, and Air Pockets.*

### Decorations

Before the party, make a selection of kites in different colours, shapes and sizes, with lots of help from the host and possibly the host's friends too. Paper kites are inexpensive and quick to make. If you enjoy sewing, try making fabric kites from brightly coloured polyester, using wire and bamboo for framing. Use these to decorate the party area. You can give these away at the end of the party as prizes, or keep some aside for Christmas or birthday gifts.

From kite to kite, fly coloured paper streamers, and hang bunches of balloons where the breeze will catch them so that they bob and rustle. A small electric fan, placed safely on a shelf, will keep streamers and balloons moving too. A rainbow, painted on butcher's paper, makes an effective backdrop.

Straw baskets containing the makings for kites — scissors, glue, rolls of tissue and coloured paper, strips of light bamboo cut to size, adhesive tape and string — will be needed later in the party and will help set the scene from the start.

### Food

The menu offers High Flying Kites, Kite Tails, Swirls and Twists, Reels of String, Smooth Landings, Clouds and Air Pockets.

**Cake:** make a Kite cake.

### Games

Arrange a *String hunt* for guests as they arrive. Collect all the string afterwards and re-use it for flying kites later.

Clear a good floor area, and have a kite-making session as soon as all the guests have assembled. Younger children may need a little help; for this age group, it is easiest to have the kite-paper cut to size, and twists of tail tissue prepared beforehand. Older children will be much more adventurous. The kites you made for party decorations will be a source of inspiration. Some children might want to make two or three different kites.

If the children are old enough, have a competition to see who can invent the most novel kite, or whose kite is the most decorative.

While the glue is drying, have a game of *Balloon dress-ups*, or play *Find the bell-ringer*.

Before going out kite-flying, serve the party food, keeping the cake aside for your return.

Take some of the kites you made as decorations to the park too, in case a couple of the kites made by guests prove to be aerodynamically disastrous.

At the park, have kite-flying competitions; whose kite can fly highest, or longest? Have a kite race. Try sending messages up the kite strings.

On your return home, serve the cake and nibbles.

### Prizes and Party Favours

The kites you made, balloons, small wind-chimes, whistles, blow-out streamers.

*Reels of String*

### REELS OF STRING

*Preparation time:* 30 minutes
*Cooking time:* 15 minutes
*Makes about 40*
*Easy*

750 g cocktail frankfurters
1 sheet frozen puff pastry, thawed
milk
tomato sauce for serving

1. Preheat oven to 180°C. Cut between frankfurters to separate and set aside. Brush pastry with a little milk. Cut into strips about 5 mm x 10 cm.
2. Wrap pastry around each frankfurter and secure with a toothpick at each end.
3. Place on an ungreased baking tray. Bake for 10–15 minutes or until pastry is golden. Serve with tomato sauce.

HINT
These can be prepared in advance, and frozen in their uncooked state.

Just before the party, remove them from the freezer and bake them.

It is best to remove toothpicks first if serving them to very young children.

## SWIRLS AND TWISTS

*Preparation time:* 20 minutes
*Cooking time:* 15 minutes
*Makes 32*
*Easy*

2 sheets frozen puff pastry, thawed
¼ cup tomato sauce
1 cup shredded tasty cheese
milk

1.  Preheat oven to 200°C. Brush one sheet of pastry with tomato sauce. Sprinkle with cheese. Place remaining sheet of pastry on top. Roll lightly with a rolling pin to seal sheets together. Brush with milk.
2.  Cut pastry into 16 strips. Cut each strip in half. Twist each piece several times. Place on an ungreased baking tray and bake for 10–15 minutes or until golden brown.

*Swirls and Twists*

*Clouds*

## CLOUDS

*Preparation time:* 20 minutes
*Cooking time:* 2 minutes
*Makes about 24*
*Easy*

250 g vegetable fat
3 cups Rice Crispies
1 cup icing sugar, sifted
1 cup desiccated coconut
1 cup dried milk powder
assorted sweets for decoration

1.  Soften vegetable fat over low heat until just melted. Combine remaining ingredients and pour over vegetable fat. Mix well together.
2.  Spoon into small paper cake cases. Decorate as desired, or leave plain. Chill until set. Keep refrigerated until required.

HINT
For a delicious variation, add chopped dried fruit or glacé cherries, sultanas or raisins to the Clouds before chilling.

41

*Smooth Landings*

*High Flying Kites*

### HIGH FLYING KITES

*Preparation time*: 1 hour plus 20
  minutes chilling time
*Cooking time*: 10 minutes per batch
*Makes about 30*
*Easy*

125 g butter
½ cup sugar
1 egg
½ teaspoon cinnamon
1½ cups plain flour
2 tablespoons cornflour
100 g marshmallows
100 g chocolate
2 x 10 cm lengths licorice
1 cup glacé icing to decorate
food colouring

1.  Preheat oven to 220°C and grease
an oven tray. Cream butter and sugar
together until pale, light and fluffy.
Beat in egg until mixture is smooth
and creamy. Sift together cinnamon,
plain flour and cornflour. Add to
butter mixture, and mix well with a

flat-bladed knife. Form mixture into a
ball. Chill covered in the refrigerator
for 20 minutes.
2.  Roll out dough on a lightly floured
board to 5 mm thick. Cut dough into
diamond shapes of equal size.
Arrange on prepared tray and bake
for 8–10 minutes or until biscuits are
a pale golden brown. Remove from
oven and cool on tray.
3.  Place marshmallows and chocolate
in a heatproof bowl. Place over
simmering water and stir over a low
heat until melted.
Cut licorice into 10 cm lengths.
Spread the underside of half the
biscuits with a little chocolate mixture
and place a piece of licorice on a
pointed edge of the biscuit to
represent the tail of the kite.
4.  Decorate the top of the remaining
biscuits with glacé icing tinted several
colours. Place in the oven (180°C) for
5 minutes to set. Remove from oven
and cool slightly prior to joining
biscuit halves.

### SMOOTH LANDINGS

*Preparation time*: 5 minutes
*Cooking time*: nil
*Serves 8*
*Easy*

4 small ripe bananas
2 cups milk
2½ cups crushed ice
½ cup passionfruit pulp

1.  Slice banana and place in a
blender bowl. Add milk and ice, and
blend for 1 minute.
2.  Add passionfruit pulp and blend
for 15 seconds. Pour into tumblers
and serve immediately.

*Kite Tails*

## AIR POCKETS

*Preparation time:* 5 minutes
*Cooking time:* 5 minutes
*Makes 8 cups*
*Easy*

⅓ cup oil
½ cup uncooked popcorn
1 clove garlic, crushed
2 tablespoons grated romano or
    parmesan cheese
½ teaspoon onion salt
¼ teaspoon dried oregano
¼ teaspoon dried basil

1.  Heat oil in a large pan. Add all the popcorn. Cover and cook, shaking pan, until popcorn stops popping.
2.  Combine all remaining ingredients. Toss popcorn in the mixture. Serve freshly made in individual bags or cups.

*Air Pockets*

## KITE TAILS

*Preparation time:* 20 minutes
*Cooking time:* 15 minutes
*Makes 50*
*Easy*

1 x 375 g packet prunes
125g mozzarella, cut into 1 cm pieces
13 rashers rindless bacon, cut into
    5 cm lengths
toothpicks (omit for younger children)

1.  Remove stones from prunes. Insert a piece of cheese in the centre of each prune. Wrap in a piece of bacon. Secure with toothpicks.
2.  Refrigerate until required. Bake at 180°C for 10–15 minutes or until bacon is crisp and cheese melts.

*Kite Cake*

## KITE CAKE

*Preparation time:* 45 minutes
*Cooking time:* 40 minutes
*Easy*

1 x 350 g packet cake mix or
    1 quantity butter cake batter
    (see page 96)
2 quantities buttercream frosting
    (see page 96)
food colouring
licorice straps
ribbon

1.  Preheat oven to 180°C and grease and line an 18 x 28 cm shallow tin. Make the cake according to directions on the packet or following recipe. Pour mixture into prepared tin and spread evenly. Bake for 30–40 minutes or until cooked. Stand 5 minutes before removing from tin. Cool.
2.  Divide frosting into four equal portions. Colour each portion differently.
3.  Cut cake to form a diamond-shaped kite as shown in diagram. Slit cake horizontally in half. Spread the bottom half of the cake with a quarter of the frosting using alternating colours. Top with second half of cake. Cut 2 x 20 cm x 1 cm strips of licorice. Push into frosting in the centre of cake, inserting it at pointed edge of the diamond.
4.  Place on a large board. Cover sides and top of cake with frosting, alternating colours. Place a strip of licorice lengthways down the centre of the cake and another strip widthways across the centre. Trim licorice so it extends 1 cm beyond edge of cake.
5.  Tie bows from ribbons and attach to the kite tail and corners of the kite cake.

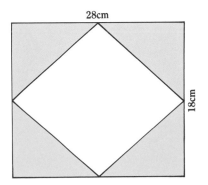

# Spooky Party

THIS IS a very easy and popular party idea and costumes are no problem. Even the shyest child will enjoy dressing up for this occasion. Inexpensive all-black costumes can be created for magicians, witches, black cats, bats, spiders, or skeletons with the bones painted in white. Easy all-white outfits made with sheets might be for ghosts and mummies. More elaborate costumes could be created for vampires, Frankensteins and devils. Hideous masks and other delightful accessories can be bought from newsagents and party speciality shops, or made by guests.

This theme can be adapted: have a Monster Party, Mask Party or Halloween Party instead, on the same lines. For Halloween, make grinning lamps out of hollowed-out pumpkins with candles inside them.

**Age group:** six to ten
**Venue:** house, garden or garage
**Number of guests:** up to 12

### Invitations
Draw a skeleton on black card, or cut out a haunted house, owl or ghost shape. Include a reminder to wear something spooky.

### Decorations
Drape the table in dark grey. Provide grey, silver or black paper plates and cups. Use spray-on cobwebbing where it won't affect the food. Encourage a spooky atmosphere with green or dim lighting. Candles and sparklers add a good effect, but remember to put them safely out of harm's way. Suspend cut-outs of spiders, owls, witches and lanterns from the ceiling. Use black balloons. Make a few ghosts from white sheets draped on coathangers: add black felt eyes, and hang them in dark corners.

If you want to use dry ice to create smoky effects, remember that dry ice **must** be kept safely out of reach at all times, as it causes very severe burning and skin damage. Under no circumstances should dry ice be touched with bare hands.

### Food
Bleeding Fingers; Broomsticks; Bites that go Crunch in the Night; Mouse Traps; Skeleton Ribs; Squelch and Crunch; Frozen Black and Goo; Ghostmallows; Vampire Blood.

**Cake:** a Halloween cake. Use 'magic' candles that die out for a few seconds then re-light themselves again.

### Games
Play *Murder in the dark*, *Wrap the mummy*, *Blind man's bluff*, *Sardines*, *Musical torch*, *Hangman*, *Guess in the dark*, and *Taste and guess*.

### Prizes and Party Favours
Inexpensive tricks from magic shops such as fake blood and dracula teeth. Rats and snakes (the jujube variety, sold in most sweet shops at a low cost).

## MOUSE TRAPS

*Preparation time:* 15 minutes
*Cooking time:* 5 minutes
*Serves 10*
*Easy*

10 slices bread
butter for spreading
Vegemite or Marmite
250 g cheese, finely grated
5 tablespoons tomato sauce

1.  Preheat grill on high. Toast bread on both sides. Spread thinly with

butter and Vegemite or Marmite. Sprinkle with grated cheese. Spoon 2 teaspoons of tomato sauce on top of cheese.
2.  Place under hot grill and cook until cheese melts and tomato sauce spreads. Serve immediately.

*Clockwise from left: Frozen Black and Goo, Broomsticks, Skeleton Ribs, Vampire Blood, Mouse Traps, Bleeding Fingers, Squelch and Crunch. Centre: Bites that go Crunch in the Night and Ghostmallows.*

*Ghostmallows*

*Broomsticks*

drain immediately. Cut each frankfurter into four pieces. Insert a pretzel into each frankfurter and set aside.

2. Combine cheese and tomato sauce in a pan. Melt over very low heat.

3. To serve: dip frankfurter 'brooms' into melted cheese mixture.

## GHOSTMALLOWS

*Preparation time:* 25 minutes
*Cooking time:* 10 minutes
*Makes about 25*
*Easy*

2 cups white sugar
6 teaspoons liquid glucose
6 teaspoons gelatine
1½ cups water
10 cups cornflour (only used for moulding, so the cornflour can be re-used)
peppermint essence, optional
licorice shapes for decoration

1. Place sugar, glucose, gelatine and water in a pan and bring to the boil. Boil 2 minutes, remove from the heat and cool.

2. Place cornflour in a deep baking dish and pack in very firmly. Make indentations in the cornflour using a single egg (a hard-boiled one is easier to use since there is less chance of breaking). Alternatively, use a small bowl to form indentations.

3. Add essence to sugar syrup. Beat with an electric mixer for 10 minutes or until mixture is thick, white and frothy. Spoon mixture into recesses in cornflour. Allow to set. Lift out of cornflour and attach small pieces of licorice to represent eyes. This is best done with a little icing if you have any left over, otherwise a dab of jam or unset marshmallow mixture will do the trick.

## BROOMSTICKS

*Preparation time:* 20 minutes
*Cooking time:* 5 minutes
*Makes 24*
*Easy*

6 frankfurters
24 pretzels
1 cup grated cheese
¼ cup tomato sauce

1. Place frankfurters in a pan of cold water. Bring just to boiling point and

## BITES THAT GO CRUNCH IN THE NIGHT

*Preparation time:* 50 minutes
*Cooking time:* 20 minutes
*Serves 10*
*Medium*

250 g pumpkin, peeled and seeds removed
1 sweet potato, peeled
2 carrots, peeled
2 potatoes, peeled
oil for frying
garlic powder

1. Using a potato peeler or a sharp paring knife, peel off paper-thin slices of vegetables. Place vegetables on a large clean tea-towel or absorbent paper and pat gently to dry.

2. Heat oil in a deep-fryer until oil sizzles when tested with a piece of vegetable. Drop in a few pieces of vegetable at a time and fry until crisp and golden. Lift out of oil and drain on absorbent paper. Repeat with remaining vegetable slices. While still

hot, sprinkle liberally with garlic powder. Serve warm or store in an airtight container until required.

VARIATIONS
These are scrumptious when sprinkled with cinnamon sugar or dusted with a light sprinkling of icing sugar, instead of garlic powder.

## SKELETON RIBS

*Preparation time:* 15 minutes plus overnight marinating time
*Cooking time:* 1 hour
*Serves 6*
*Easy*

2 racks beef ribs

MARINADE
⅔ cup soy sauce
juice of 2 lemons
2 teaspoons freshly grated ginger
¼ cup grainy mustard
½ cup brown sugar
6 shallots, chopped
1 cup tomato purée
pinch pepper

1. Mix together all ingredients for marinade and pour over ribs. Cover and marinate overnight in the refrigerator.
2. To cook ribs: place on a rack in a roasting pan. Brush or spoon marinade over ribs. Barbecue or bake at 200°C for 45 minutes–1 hour, basting frequently. Serve hot.

*Bleeding Fingers*

*Skeleton Ribs*

## BLEEDING FINGERS

*Preparation time:* 20 minutes
*Cooking time:* 1 hour
*Makes 20*
*Medium*

2 egg whites
½ cup white sugar
1 cup desiccated coconut
½ cup raspberry or strawberry jam

1. Preheat oven to 150°C. Line a baking tray with baking paper or grease and dust liberally with cornflour.
2. Beat egg whites until stiff peaks form. Beat in sugar, one tablespoon at a time, and continue beating until mixture is thick and glossy. Fold through coconut. Fit a piping bag with a plain 2 cm tube and fill it with the meringue mixture. Pipe 8 cm lengths onto prepared tray.
3. Bake in oven for 5 minutes, reduce heat to 130°C and cook for a further 45–50 minutes until fingers are dry and crispy. Turn off oven and leave meringues to cool.
4. In a pan heat jam over low heat

until thin and runny. Remove meringues from tray in oven and dip into jam, allowing excess to drip away. Place on a rack to cool.

## VAMPIRE BLOOD

*Preparation time:* 10 minutes
*Cooking time:* 10 minutes
*Makes 2 litres*
*Easy*

1.25 litres water
1.5 kg sugar
30 g citric acid
2 teaspoons raspberry essence
few drops red food colouring (optional)

1. Heat water and sugar in a pan, to boiling point, stirring until sugar is dissolved. Boil for 5 minutes.
2. Pour into a large jug, add citric acid and stir until dissolved. Set aside until cold. Stir in raspberry essence and a little food colouring if you wish. Pour into sterilised bottles. Serve 1 tablespoon of cordial diluted with iced water to taste.

*Frozen Black and Goo*

## FROZEN BLACK AND GOO

*Preparation time:* 30 minutes plus
   freezing time
*Cooking time:* nil
*Serves 10*
*Easy*

1 litre vanilla ice-cream
50 g chocolate chips or pieces
3 tablespoons chocolate-flavoured
   syrup
1 x 250 g punnet strawberries, hulled
   and chopped
3 tablespoons strawberry-flavoured
   syrup
100 g pink and white marshmallows
8 small wooden ice-cream sticks

1.  Soften ice-cream at room
temperature until soft but still firm.
Divide ice-cream into thirds. Into the
first third mix chocolate chips and

chocolate syrup. Spoon evenly into
eight waxed paper cups. Place in
freezer.
2.  Into the second third add
strawberries and strawberry syrup.
Spoon evenly on top of the chocolate
mixture. Return cups to freezer.
3.  Into the remaining ice-cream mix
the marshmallows. Spoon on top of
the strawberry and chocolate mixture
in cups. Insert an ice-cream stick and
freeze for a minimum of three hours
to set firm. Peel waxed cups away
from ice-cream and replace in freezer
to harden.

HINT
It is important to use a good quality
ice-cream for this recipe, since the
lesser quality ice-creams tend to
become runny very quickly after
softening.

## SQUELCH AND CRUNCH

*Preparation time:* 30 minutes
*Cooking time:* 40 minutes
*Makes 18–20*
*Medium*

BISCUIT BASE
1 cup brown sugar, firmly packed
1 egg
2 cups self-raising flour
2 tablespoons cocoa
125 g butter
2 tablespoons milk

MARSHMALLOW TOPPING
½ cup sugar
2 teaspoons gelatine
½ cup water
1 teaspoon vanilla essence
green food colouring (optional)
silver cachous

1.  Preheat oven to 180°C. Lightly
grease a flat oven tray. Mix together
sugar, egg and half the flour and
cocoa, sifted together. Melt butter
over gentle heat. Stir in milk and pour
into the dry ingredients.
2.  Beat well for 2–3 minutes. Add the
rest of the sifted dry ingredients and
mix well. Take small portions, roll
into balls and arrange on prepared
trays. Press down with a fork and
bake for about 15 minutes or until
lightly browned. Cool.
3.  To prepare topping: combine
sugar, gelatine and water in a small
pan. Stir over low heat until boiling.
Simmer, without stirring, for 3–4
minutes, then cool.

*Squelch and Crunch*

4. Stir in vanilla essence and colouring. Beat with an electric beater until thick and fluffy. Spoon on top of biscuits and decorate with silver cachous.

NOTE
Do not top the biscuits with marshmallow until the day they are to be eaten, because they will soften.

## HALLOWEEN CAKE

*Preparation time:* 1½ hours
*Cooking time:* 45 minutes
*Medium*

2 x 350 g packets cake mix or
   2 quantities butter cake batter
   (see page 96)
jam
1 quantity butter icing (see page 96)
¼ teaspoon grated orange rind
orange food colouring
almond paste
yellow food colouring
licorice

1. Preheat oven to 180°C. Grease 2 metal jelly moulds. These must be 3-cup capacity and should be vertically ribbed. Make the cake according to directions on the packet or following recipe. Turn into prepared moulds and bake for 40–45 minutes or until cooked. Cool.
2. Level the top of each cake and spread the cut surface with jam. Sandwich the two cakes together. Place on a cake rack.
3. To prepare topping: add orange rind and orange food colouring to butter icing. Cover the cake completely (see diagram 1). Knead the almond paste until soft, and work in a little yellow food colouring. Mould a top and stem for the pumpkin. Place these on the cake. Cut licorice shapes for a face and fasten them to the cake, using some of the icing (see diagrams).

NOTE
If no vertically ribbed jelly moulds are available, bake two cakes in plain 3-cup capacity pudding basins, and cut vertical serrations in them to provide a pumpkin effect.

*Halloween Cake*

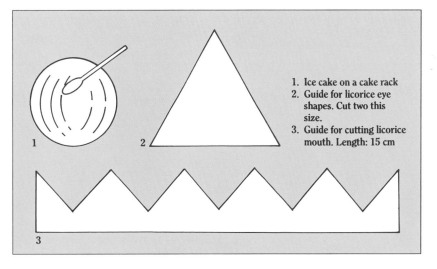

1. Ice cake on a cake rack
2. Guide for licorice eye shapes. Cut two this size.
3. Guide for cutting licorice mouth. Length: 15 cm

# Space Party

THIS IS ALWAYS a very popular party theme for young children. Many children have remnants from past presents or events to create a costume. Costumes can also be made from boxes, paper, silver foil or packing oddments like polystyrene chips. Children could dress as space creatures, Martians, astronauts or spacecraft. Florist's wire makes good antennae and a small box, covered in foil, makes a convincing hand-held transmitter.

**Age group:** six to ten
**Venue:** garage or basement
**Number of guests:** up to 12

### Invitations
A flying saucer made from two paper plates, joined by a single staple at the side. Invite your guests to board the Intergalactic Starship for a trip to the Outer Nebulae.

### Decorations
Cover the party table with butcher's paper, then place a layer of dark blue cellophane over that. The effect is a deep translucent blue. Scatter silver foil stars or comet's tail streamers across the table top. Float silver or black balloons from the ceiling. Make paper stars, suns, and planets, paint or colour them and add sprinklings of glitter; hang these from light fittings, curtain tracks and the tops of doors. Cover the windows with blue or green cellophane to filter the daylight, or put cellophane covers over the light fittings for unearthly light effects. (Remember to keep the cellophane a safe distance from the bulb itself.) Cut comets and asteroids from silver foil, to pin up on the walls.

### Food
Star Dust, Outer Space Shapes, Galactic Discs, Moon Rocks, Meteors, Space Wheels, Foaming Craters, Space Spuds, Moon Moguls, Moon Buggy Wheels.

**Cake:** the Outer Space Cake will fill inner spaces.

### Games
Make a cassette of space music before the party, and use this for music games. Play *Guess in the dark*, *Magpies*, the *Flour game*, *Hedgehogs*, *Mystery matchboxes*. Or play a variation of *What's the Time, Mr Wolf?* with a change of title — *What's the time, Darth Vader?*

*I Went to Mars* is a popular and challenging game. The first child announces: 'I went to Mars, and I took a . . .' and names any object — 'I went to Mars, and I took a pencil.' The next one has to repeat the object and add another. 'I went to Mars and I took a pencil and an apple.' The third will add a new object, always keeping the list in order: 'I went to Mars, and I took a pencil, an apple and my dog.' Turns continue around the circle for as long as possible.

### Prizes and Party Favours
Small magic tricks, packets of glittery stars (available from most stationers), bubble pipes, novelty straws, and star dust (sherbet).

## FOAMING CRATERS

*Preparation time:* 10 minutes
*Cooking time:* nil
*Serves 8*
*Easy*

1 x 250 g punnet strawberries, washed
   and hulled
8 large scoops vanilla ice-cream
2 x 750 ml bottles lemonade

*Foaming Craters*

1. Purée strawberries until smooth. Divide purée evenly between eight tall tumblers.
2. Place a scoop of ice-cream in each glass and top with lemonade, being careful mixture does not overflow. Serve immediately.

*Clockwise from top left: Space Wheels, Moon Buggy Wheels, Foaming Craters, Moon Moguls, Star Dust, Galactic Discs, Meteors, Space Spuds, Outer Space Shapes and Moon Rocks.*

a further 20 minutes or until 'wheels' are golden and crispy to touch. Remove from oven and cool on a wire rack.

5. Whip cream with sugar and vanilla until thick. Crumble Flake bar and chop Violet Crumble or honeycomb bars into spiky-shaped chunks.

6. To assemble: halve wheels horizontally. Scrape out any moist mixture in the centre. Spoon or pipe whipped cream into the cavity, and top with spikes of chocolate and honeycomb bars.

## MOON ROCKS

*Preparation time:* 15 minutes
*Cooking time:* 30 minutes
*Makes 24*
*Medium*

2 cups white crystal sugar
300 ml water
4 tablespoons malt vinegar
½ teaspoon bicarbonate of soda

1. Line 2 deep muffin trays with 24 paper cake cases. Place sugar, water and vinegar in a large pan, bring slowly to the boil and stir until sugar dissolves. Wash any sugar crystals down the sides of the pan with a wet brush before mixture boils.

2. Boil rapidly without stirring until

*Space Wheels*

*Moon Rocks*

## SPACE WHEELS

*Preparation time:* 45 minutes
*Cooking time:* 40 minutes
*Makes 24*
*Medium*

1 cup water
125 g butter, cut into small pieces
1 cup plain flour, sifted
3 eggs, beaten
300 ml thickened cream
1 tablespoon sugar
1 teaspoon vanilla essence
1 x 30 g bar Flake or chocolate bar
2 x 45 g bars Violet Crumble or
    chocolate-coated honeycomb

1. Preheat oven to 190°C. Lightly grease a baking tray and mark 10 cm circles on the tray.

2. Place water and butter in a pan and bring to the boil. Add flour all at once and immediately beat until smooth with no lumps remaining. Return to heat and cook over low heat for 2–3 minutes or until mixture leaves the sides of the pan. Remove from heat and cool slightly.

3. Beat in egg a little at a time, beating well between additions. When all the egg has been added, the mixture should be glossy and thick enough to have a wooden spoon stand up in it.

4. Fit a piping bag with a plain 2 cm tube and fill it with mixture. Pipe around edge of marked rounds to give doughnut shapes. Bake for 20 minutes or until 'wheels' puff. Reduce heat to 160°C and continue cooking

mixture starts to change colour and turns golden. Remove from heat immediately and stand 2 minutes.

3.  Add bicarbonate of soda and stir through toffee mixture. The mixture will froth up immediately so it is important to use a pan large enough to allow for the expansion. Pour frothing mixture into prepared trays and stand at room temperature until set and crisp.

## METEORS

*Preparation time:* 40 minutes
*Cooking time:* 10 minutes
*Makes about 40*
*Medium*

1 cup water
125 g butter, cut into small pieces
1 cup plain flour, sifted
3 eggs, lightly beaten
2 tablespoons sugar
½ teaspoon cinnamon
oil for deep-frying

COATING MIXTURE
1 cup caster sugar
1 teaspoon cinnamon
1 teaspoon nutmeg

1.  Place water and butter in a pan and bring to the boil. Add the flour all at once and beat immediately until smooth with no lumps remaining. Return to heat and stir over low heat for 2–3 minutes or until the mixture leaves the sides of the pan. Cool slightly.

2.  Beat in egg, a little at a time, until mixture becomes smooth and glossy. Combine sugar and ½ teaspoon cinnamon, and stir this evenly through the mixture.

3.  Heat oil in a deep-fryer. The oil will be hot enough when a 2 cm cube of bread becomes golden brown in 20 seconds when dropped into it. Spoon teaspoonfuls of the mixture into hot oil. Fry for 1–2 minutes or until golden brown, puffed and cooked through. Drain well on absorbent paper.

4.  Prepare coating mixture by combining ingredients in a bowl. Toss hot puffs in coating and serve immediately while still warm.

*Outer Space Shapes*

## OUTER SPACE SHAPES

*Preparation time:* 1 hour plus 20 minutes chilling time
*Cooking time:* 10 minutes per batch
*Makes about 30*
*Easy*

125 g butter
½ cup sugar
1 egg
½ teaspoon cinnamon
1½ cups plain flour
2 tablespoons cornflour
100 g marshmallows
100 g chocolate
2 x 10 cm lengths licorice
1 cup glacé icing to decorate
food colouring

1.  Preheat oven to 220°C and grease an oven tray. Cream butter and sugar together until pale, light and fluffy. Beat in egg until mixture is smooth and creamy. Sift together cinnamon, plain flour and cornflour. Add to butter mixture, and mix well with a flat-bladed knife. Form mixture into a ball. Chill covered in the refrigerator for 20 minutes.

2.  Roll out dough on a lightly floured board to 5 mm thick. Cut dough into star and moon shapes of similar size. Arrange on prepared tray and bake for 8–10 minutes or until biscuits are a pale golden brown. Remove from oven and cool on tray.

3.  Place marshmallows and chocolate in a heatproof bowl. Place over simmering water and stir over a low heat until melted. Spread the underside of half the biscuits with a little chocolate mixture.

4.  Decorate the top of the remaining biscuits with glacé icing, tinted several colours. Place in oven at 180°C for 5 minutes to set. Remove from oven and cool slightly prior to joining identical biscuit halves.

53

cook 1 minute. Remove from heat. Gradually blend in milk a little at a time, beating until smooth. Stir over medium heat until boiling; boil for 3 minutes. Remove from heat.

3. Stir in mayonnaise, half the cheese, then corn and ham. Spoon mixture into vol-au-vent cases and sprinkle with remaining cheese. Heat in oven for 10 minutes until cheese is melted and the filling is hot.

*Star Dust*

## GALACTIC DISCS

*Preparation time:* 10 minutes
*Cooking time:* 8 minutes
*Makes 12*
*Easy*

12 gingernut biscuits
12 white marshmallows
24 licorice straws
12 Smarties

1. Preheat oven to 150°C. Line a muffin tray with 12 paper cake cases, and place a gingernut biscuit in each case. Top with a marshmallow. Heat in the oven for 5 minutes, or until biscuit softens and takes on the shape of the container and marshmallow softens slightly.

2. Remove from the oven and immediately insert 2 licorice sticks into each marshmallow as antennae; place a Smartie in the centre.

NOTE
If marshmallow sets prior to inserting licorice, either return it to the oven for a minute more or attach the licorice with a little icing or frosting.

*Galactic Discs*

## STAR DUST

*Preparation time:* 15 minutes
*Cooking time:* nil
*Serves 10*
*Easy*

3 cups icing sugar
1 teaspoon food colouring
2 x 25 g packet Fruit Tingles or acid drops
¼ teaspoon bicarbonate of soda
½ teaspoon cream of tartar
1 teaspoon citric acid
10 licorice straws

1. Place sugar into a large bag, add a few drops of food colouring and shake bag vigorously until sugar is evenly coloured. Transfer to a large bowl.

2. Place Fruit Tingles or acid drops into a food processor or blender and process until finely chopped. Add to icing sugar with bicarbonate of soda, cream of tartar and citric acid. Mix well until ingredients are evenly distributed.

3. Spoon into individual bags and add a licorice straw through which to suck sherbet mixture.

## MOON MOGULS

*Preparation time:* 25 minutes
*Cooking time:* 15 minutes
*Serves 10*
*Easy*

10 x 8 cm precooked vol-au-vent cases
40 g butter
2 tablespoons plain flour
1 cup milk
1 tablespoon mayonnaise
125 g cheese, grated
1 cup corn niblets, cooked
125 g ham, finely chopped

1. Preheat oven to 180°C. Place vol-au-vent cases onto a flat ungreased oven tray.

2. Melt butter in pan, lift off heat and stir in flour. Return to low heat and

## MOON BUGGY WHEELS

*Preparation time:* 15 minutes
*Cooking time:* nil
*Serves 10*
*Easy*

10 bagels
butter
10 round slices ham
20 cherry tomatoes, halved
20 green cocktail onions, halved
toothpicks (omit for younger children)

1. Slit bagels horizontally in half.
Spread lightly with butter. Place a
slice of ham on one half of each
bagel, top with second half of the
bagel.
2. Insert a toothpick into a tomato
half and top with a green cocktail
onion. Arrange 4 tomato and onion
'bolts' around the edge of each bagel.
Serve.

## SPACE SPUDS

*Preparation time:* 40 minutes
*Cooking time:* 1 hour 10 minutes
*Serves 10*
*Easy*

5 large potatoes
heavy duty foil
2 tablespoons sour cream
20 g butter
1 egg
1 tablespoon mayonnaise
1 tablespoon chopped chives
3 seafood sticks, finely sliced
125 g tasty cheese

1. Preheat oven to 190°C. Wash
potatoes until skin is clean and free of
dirt, then wrap them tightly in heavy
duty foil. Bake for 1 hour or until
tender when pierced with a skewer.
Remove from oven and allow to stand
until cool enough to handle.
2. Cut potatoes in half, leaving foil
intact. Scoop out flesh with a metal
spoon and mash until smooth. Beat in
cream, butter, egg, mayonnaise and
chives. Stir the seafood stick slice
through the potato mixture.
3. Spoon mixture back into potato
halves, top with cheese and heat in
oven for 10 minutes until cheese is
melted and lightly browned.

*Outer Space Cake*

## OUTER SPACE CAKE

*Preparation time:* 40 minutes
*Cooking time:* 50 minutes
*Easy*

1 x 350 g packet cake mix or 1 quantity
    butter cake batter (see page 96)
500 g cream cheese, softened
¼ cup sifted icing sugar
1 teaspoon vanilla
a little milk if necessary
redcurrant jelly or raspberry jam
aluminium foil
toothpicks
red sweets
pipe cleaners
2 small space figures

1. Preheat oven to 180°C. Grease,
line and grease again a 20 cm round
cake tin. Make the cake according to
directions on the packet or following
recipe. Pour mixture into prepared tin
and bake for 50 minutes or until
cooked. Cool. Place cake on board.
2. Beat cheese until very soft and
creamy. Beat in icing sugar and
vanilla. If necessary, beat in a little
milk to give a spreading consistency.
3. Swirl mixture over cake, building
up peaks and craters as pictured.
Make a 'river' with jelly or jam.
4. Use two balls of crumpled foil for
the spaceship body. Fold strips of foil
concertina fashion for the steps.
Cover 3 toothpicks with foil for
antennae, and stick a red sweet on the
end of each. Cover pipe cleaners with
foil, and bend into position to make
the legs of the spaceship. Place space
figures in position.

# Character Party

T HIS PARTY IS built around the theme of a favourite nursery rhyme, book or movie. The chosen title will provide a variety of ideas for fancy dress, and can be adapted to suit most age groups. Characters to dress as could include traditional or current favourites — Robin Hood, Snow White, Sherlock Holmes, Mowgli or any recent movie hero.

**Age group:** six to ten
**Venue:** house or garage
**Number of guests:** up to 12

### Invitations
Make a mask card, or buy a packet of paper masks and write the invitation on the back of each one. Ask your guests to come dressed as their favourite character. As a passport to the party, ask guests to bring a self-portrait of their character.

### Decorations
A few weeks before the party, start collecting old magazines and coloured newspaper supplements featuring pop or movie stars. Pin these up around the party area. Make a banner on a sheet of butcher's paper, announcing the Hall of Fame, and hang that over the door or on the gate. As the guests arrive, hang their passport portraits around the walls.

Pin up a large piece of blank butcher's paper on one wall, and have a bowl of mixed poster paint nearby. Have arriving guests 'sign in' to the Hall of Fame by dipping their hands in the paint, making a hand print on the paper, and then signing their characters' names beneath. (If the bowl of paint is placed on newspaper, and you have a wet facecloth and a bowl of clean water nearby, hands can be quickly cleaned afterwards.)

Paper plates, cups, and matching paper tablecloths featuring current movie heroes or Disney characters are available from speciality party shops.

### Food
Batwing Biscuits, Superman Sausages, Mickey Munchies, Snow White Surprise, Melon Jaws, Bluebeard's Bundles, and Mad Hatter Punch.

**Cake:** a Rupert Bear cake.

### Games
Use music from a popular movie to play games such as *Pass the parcel*, *Jump the broom*, *Musical statues* and *Musical chairs*. Play the *Chocolate game* or have a *Guessing competition*.

Play *Partners*. Before the party, draw up a list of famous partners — Miss Piggy and Kermit, Robin Hood and Maid Marion, Peter Pan and Wendy, and so on. Write each name on a piece of paper. At the start of the game, pin a name on the back of each child, not allowing them to see their own names. Then each child must establish who he or she is, by asking questions of the other players. ('Am I an animal? What colour am I?') Answers should be given in the form of clues — 'You're green' — without giving away the name, until players arrive at the right identity. Once each child has correctly guessed who they are, they then search for their partners, whose names, of course, they can see.

### Prizes and Party Favours
Badges, party whistles, small puzzle games.

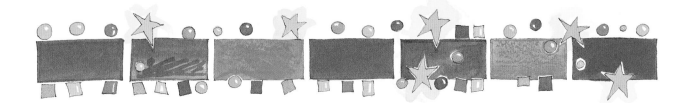

## SNOW WHITE SURPRISE

*Preparation time:* 30 minutes plus
  30 minutes freezing time
*Cooking time:* nil
*Serves 10*
*Easy*

2 litres vanilla ice-cream
10 white marshmallows
10 thin strips of licorice
20 Smarties
4 glacé cherries, cut into quarters

1. Using a large ice-cream scoop,
place 10 scoops of ice-cream on a flat
tray. Make 10 more scoops using a

small scoop. Place these on top of
large scoops. Freeze for 30 minutes to
become firm.
2. Remove from freezer and top each
one with a marshmallow for a hat. Tie
licorice around 'neck' to form a scarf.
Place Smarties on small scoops of ice-
cream for eyes and add one-quarter of
a glacé cherry for the mouth. Return
to freezer until ready to serve.

*Clockwise from left: Mickey Munchies,
Superman Sausages, Melon Jaws, Mad
Hatter's Punch, Snow White Surprise,
Bluebeard's Bundles, and Bat Wing Biscuits.*

## BLUEBEARD'S BUNDLES

*Preparation time:* 1 hour
*Cooking time:* 25 minutes
*Makes 40*
*Medium*

125 g uncooked prawns, shelled,
    deveined and finely chopped
250 g chicken mince
1 small carrot, finely chopped
4 cups finely chopped spring onions or
    shallots
1 tablespoon soy sauce
2 tablespoons fish sauce
pinch pepper
about 40 fresh (or frozen and thawed)
    won ton wrappers
vegetable or peanut oil for deep-frying
extra soy sauce for serving

1.  In a bowl combine chopped
prawns, chicken mince, carrot, spring
onions, sauces, and pepper to taste.
Mix lightly but thoroughly.
2.  Place 1 teaspoonful of the mixture
in the centre of each wonton wrapper.
Moisten edges lightly with water.
Gather up 4 corners of wrapper
together and seal.
3.  Heat about 2 cups oil in a wok or

*Bluebeard's Bundles*

*Melon Jaws*

## MELON JAWS

*Preparation time:* 20 minutes
*Cooking time:* nil
*Serves:* depends on size of melon
*Easy*

1 long oval shaped melon, chilled
2 glacé cherries, black olives or
    2 cherry tomatoes

1.  Place melon on a large tray. If
melon is not sitting firmly on tray, cut
off a thin slice underneath to give a
flat base.
2.  Mark melon with the tip of a sharp
knife to give a cutting guide. Cut out a
jagged edge to represent a mouth.
Cut a 'V' from the other end to
represent the shark's tail.
The 'V' shape that has been removed
will form the fin. Secure it to the top
of the shark's body with toothpicks or
a fine skewer.
3.  Attach 2 glacé cherries for the
shark's eyes with toothpicks. Cut into
thin slices to serve.

heavy-based pan until hot. Fry 5–6 at a time, over 3–4 minutes, turning once. Drain on paper towels. Serve hot with soy sauce for dipping.

## MAD HATTER'S PUNCH

*Preparation time:* 15 minutes plus
  chilling time
*Cooking time:* 4 minutes
*Serves 10*
*Easy*

150 ml water
1 cup sugar
1 x 850 ml can pineapple juice
1 cup orange juice
juice 2 large lemons
2 passionfruit
5 cups black tea, chilled
2 x 285 ml bottles dry ginger ale,
  chilled
fresh mint sprigs
1 cup pineapple chunks
1 ripe firm banana, sliced

1.  Heat water and sugar in a pan, stirring over gentle heat until sugar dissolves. Boil for 3 minutes. Set aside to cool.
2.  When cold, mix in fruit juices and passionfruit. Chill thoroughly. When needed, combine with tea and ginger ale in a bowl over crushed ice. Add mint sprigs, pineapple and banana slices to serve.

*Bat Wing Biscuits*

*Mad Hatter's Punch*

## BAT WING BISCUITS

*Preparation time:* 35 minutes plus
  1 hour chilling time
*Cooking time:* 10 minutes
*Makes 12*
*Easy*

90 g butter, softened
2 tablespoons golden syrup
1 tablespoon cream
¼ teaspoon almond essence
1¾ cups plain flour
strips of licorice
2 tablespoons cocoa
3 tablespoons icing sugar

1.  Preheat oven to 190°C and lightly grease a flat oven tray. Using a wooden spoon, beat together softened butter, golden syrup, cream and almond essence, and blend well. Gradually stir in flour to make a firm dough (in hot weather you may need to add a little extra flour).
2.  Knead the dough lightly until smooth. Wrap and chill in the refrigerator for 1 hour or until firm enough to handle.
3.  Roll out biscuit dough on a lightly floured board to 5 cm thickness. Cut biscuits into the shape of 'bat wings'. Press strips of licorice into biscuits to form bat 'veins'. Bake in oven for 7–10 minutes until firm and golden. Cool on tray.
4.  To serve: combine cocoa and icing sugar and sprinkle liberally through a fine strainer over the biscuits.

*Superman Sausages*

paper piping bags with mixtures. Place frankfurter on roll and pipe a blue 'S' along its length. Pipe a yellow 'S' next to the blue 'S'. Serve at once.

## MICKEY MUNCHIES

*Preparation time:* 5 minutes
*Cooking time:* nil
*Serves 10*
*Easy*

1 cup plain rice crackers
1 cup banana crisps
1 cup shredded coconut
1 cup unsalted peanuts
1 cup raisins
2 cups toasted muesli
4 cups fresh popcorn
1 cup sunflower kernels or pumpkin
　　seeds

1. Combine all ingredients in a large bowl and mix well. Spoon into individual bags or containers for serving.

*Mickey Munchies*

## SUPERMAN SAUSAGES

*Preparation time:* 25 minutes
*Cooking time:* 10 minutes
*Serves 10*
*Medium*

10 continental frankfurters
5 long bread rolls
butter for spreading
tomato sauce
1 x 200 g tub cream cheese
2 tablespoons mayonnaise
1 teaspoon mild mustard
yellow and blue food colouring

1. Place frankfurters on griller tray and cook under a hot griller for 10 minutes, turning once. The skin should have a blistered appearance and frankfurters be warmed through.
2. Slit rolls horizontally and place on a serving platter cut side up. Spread thinly with butter and liberally with tomato sauce.
3. Combine cream cheese, mayonnaise and mustard, and mix well. Tint half the mixture bright yellow and the other half blue. Fill two

## RUPERT BEAR

*Preparation time:* 1¼ hours
*Cooking time:* 40 minutes
*Easy*

2 x 350 g packets cake mix or
   2 quantities butter cake batter
   (see page 96)
½ cup coconut
3–4 tablespoons seedless jam
1½ quantities butter icing (see page 96)
yellow food colouring
red food colouring
3 licorice straps
1 chocolate button
50 g cooking chocolate

1. Preheat oven to 180°C. Grease and line two 22 x 32 cm Swiss roll tins. Make the cakes together according to directions on the packet or following recipe. Stir in coconut. Pour mixture into prepared tins and bake for 30–40 minutes. Cool before trimming the tops off to give a flat surface. Sandwich cakes together with jam.

2. Cut a paper pattern of Rupert, using diagram 4 as a guide. Using the pattern, cut a Rupert shape from the cake. Then cut the paper pattern into two pieces, separating the face from the shoulders and scarf. Remove the face pattern, leaving the shoulder and scarf pattern on the cake.

3. Ice the Rupert face (see diagram 1) with butter icing. Divide the remaining butter icing in half. Colour one part yellow and the other part red, with food colouring. Cut the scarf from the shoulder pattern, giving three pieces. Leave the two shoulder patterns on the cake, so the scarf

*Rupert Bear Cake*

shape is free for icing (see diagram 2).

4. Fill an icing bag with yellow icing. Pipe around the edges of the scarf. Fill in scarf with the remaining yellow icing.

5. Use narrow strips of licorice to make the plaid pattern on the scarf and outline it with long licorice strips.

6 Put half the red icing into a piping bag, and pipe around the edge of the scarf (see diagram 3). Spread the remaining red icing over the shoulders to give Rupert his red jersey. Use narrow strips of licorice as a nose and outline his mouth (see diagram 4). Halve the chocolate button to make two half circles for eyes. Melt the cooking chocolate and use a pastry brush to paint Rupert's chocolate mouth.

1. Cut away face from paper pattern, and ice the face.

2. Cut scarf from pattern and ice.

3. Pipe on Rupert's scarf.

4. Place licorice in position for ears, nose and mouth.

# Picnic Party

THE PARK OR local nature reserve is a great place to hold a Picnic party. Everyone can run their legs off and work up an appetite. It also solves the problem of accommodating large numbers of children if your child wants the whole class to attend. The park provides plenty of scope for outdoor team games, too. Games of tag or hide-and-seek are good. Be well prepared and have a list of chosen activities made out before you get there. If you have a very large group, you may need extra adults or teenagers to help you. It is essential to remember everything before you leave home — use the checklist.

**Age group:** six to twelve
**Venue:** park or local reserve
**Number of guests:** up to 20

### Invitations
Make a card in the shape of a soccer or cricket ball, or a sausage. Give good, clear instructions of when and where to meet. Be precise about pick-up time as many large parks close their gates at sunset. Provide an alternative should the heavens open, and ask children to bring raincoats and sunhats to cover all eventualities.

*Clockwise from left: Maggot Mounds, Bugs in Rugs, Ant Floater, The Sausage Sizzle, Porcupines, Butterfly Cakes and Insy Winsy Spiders.*

### Decorations

Bunches of balloons tied to trees and parked cars make your group easy to find. Make a banner from an old sheet, or a poster, announcing the event: 'Susan's Party', and tie it between two bushes. Take picnic rugs and multi-coloured plastic picnic ware.

### Food

Pack individual picnics with all the party trappings. If barbecues are provided, have a sausage sizzle or serve satays. Suggested menu: Insy Winsy Spiders; Porcupines; Bugs in Rugs; Ant Floaters; Maggot Mounds, and Butterfly cakes.

**Cake:** a Snake cake will be popular.

### Games

Cricket, soccer, or volley-ball; a treasure hunt, a *Tug of war*; play *Grandmother's footsteps*; *Pass the parcel*; *Overpass, underpass*; or have a *Water race*. Have a *Hot Potato Relay* and play *Sardines*.

### Prizes and Party Favours

Inexpensive skipping ropes — hand them out early if necessary. Clickers, whistles, colourful balls and badges.

## Park Checklist

*For the picnic:* a fold-up table and chairs, or rugs and ground sheets.

*For the meal:* plastic plates and cups, napkins, cutlery, sharp knife, salad bowls, tablecloth.

*Barbecue:* large serving plates and barbecue tools. Check beforehand whether you need to take along fuel, hot plate or grill. A scraper to clean the barbecue before cooking.

*Food extras:* as well as prepared party food, remember to take sauces, pepper, salt, and salad dressing. Take candles for the cake, and matches to light them.

It's very important to have enough to drink. Any extra can always be taken home, but children will consume a large amount of fruit juice, soft drinks or water, especially if the day is hot.

*Equipment:* your pre-planned games programme will remind you of the sporting equipment needed. It is a good idea to put all these items in a clothes basket so that they are together for easy finding. Remember to take a good thick rope for the tug of war. Take a loud whistle.

Take a big garbage bag for collecting waste at the end of the party. Collecting the rubbish could be organised as a team game, with the winning team being the one whose sector is tidied first.

*First Aid Equipment:* a good basic first aid kit is essential. Add to it spare toilet paper, tissues, insect repellent and sunscreen. A container of moist paper towels will be useful too.

*Safety Notes:* if the reserve is a large one where children could get lost, take 5 minutes at the start of the party to discuss safety with them. Arrange a signal that calls them back to you — three blasts on a whistle to indicate time for lunch or a team game.

Make sure children don't wander into the forest alone. A head count every now and then will alert you to strays.

*Maggot Mounds*

## MAGGOT MOUNDS

*Preparation time:* 20 minutes
*Cooking time:* 12 minutes
*Makes 40*
*Easy*

2 x 250 g packets desiccated coconut
1 x 410 g can condensed milk
2 teaspoons vanilla essence
glacé cherries and coloured sprinkles for decoration (optional)

1. Preheat oven to 180°C and grease oven trays. In a bowl combine coconut, add the condensed milk and vanilla. Mix until thoroughly combined. Drop a teaspoonful at a time on to prepared trays, leaving 2.5 cm between each mound.
2. Decorate with glacé cherries or sprinkles. Bake for 10–12 minutes, or until lightly browned. Remove from trays immediately, and cool.

## THE SAUSAGE SIZZLE

*Preparation time:* 50 minutes
*Cooking time:* 20 minutes
*Serves 10*
*Easy*

1.5 kg barbecue sausages
6 onions, finely sliced
2 teaspoons oil
60 g butter, melted

EXTRA INGREDIENTS
buttered long bread rolls
barbecue and tomato sauces
grated cheese
shredded lettuce
coleslaw
sliced tomato
shredded carrot
mayonnaise

1. Bring a large pan of water to the boil. Drop in sausages, reduce heat and cook for 5 minutes. Drain and cool. Pierce sausages with a fork or skewer.
2. Place onion slices on a large sheet of foil and drizzle a little oil and butter over them. Wrap securely. Place sausages and onions over hot coals and barbecue, turning frequently, for 10–15 minutes or until sausages are browned and onions are soft when you unwrap foil to test them.
3. To serve: place onions and sausages onto a large platter and allow guests to construct their own 'sausage roll' with the extra ingredients.

*The Sausage Sizzle*

*Insy Winsy Spiders*

## INSY WINSY SPIDER

*Preparation time:* 40 minutes
*Cooking time:* 15 minutes
*Makes 24*
*Medium*

1 x 340 g chocolate cake mix
100 g chocolate
30 g butter
4 licorice straps
3 cups shredded coconut, tinted green
½ cup glacé icing (optional)
a little grated chocolate (optional)
24 red Smarties

1. Preheat oven to temperature recommended on the cake mix packet. Grease 24 shallow muffin pans. Make up cake mix according to the directions on the pack. Fill each muffin tin two-thirds full with cake mixture. Bake for 10–15 minutes or until cooked when tested. Cool on a wire rack, rounded side facing upwards. Place a clean oven tray underneath.
2. Melt chocolate and butter in a small heatproof bowl over simmering water. Remove from heat and beat well.
3. Spoon chocolate over cakes, ensuring that each cake is completely covered. The excess that drips onto the tray underneath may be re-melted and used to pour over cakes. Allow chocolate to set.
4. Cut licorice straps into thin lengths 3 cm long. Attach eight of these lengths to each cake as spiders' legs; insert them into the cake or attach with a little glacé icing.
5. Cut Smarties in half and place cut side down in chocolate icing at one end of cake to form eyes. Arrange spiders on coconut on a large platter. If you wish, decorate with a little glacé icing to highlight spiders' features and sprinkle cakes with chocolate to make furry bodies.

*Butterfly Cakes*

## PORCUPINES

*Preparation time*: 30 minutes
*Cooking time*: 40 minutes
*Serves 8*
*Medium*

500 g minced chicken
½ cup soft white breadcrumbs
1 egg white
1 x 230 g can water chestnuts, finely
   chopped
1 clove garlic, finely chopped
6 shallots, finely chopped
1 tablespoon light soy sauce
½ teaspoon sesame oil
2 cups long grain white rice
lettuce or cabbage leaves for steaming

1. Combine chicken, breadcrumbs,
egg white, water chestnuts, garlic,
shallots, soy and sesame oil, mixing
well.
2. Using wet hands, mould mixture
into 3cm balls. Roll balls in uncooked
rice, pressing gently to make rice
stick.
3. Place rice balls in the top of a
steamer lined with lettuce leaves.
Steam over boiling water for 35–40
minutes until the rice is tender and
the meat balls are cooked through to
the centre. Serve hot or cold.

## BUTTERFLY CAKES

*Preparation time*: 40 minutes
*Cooking time*: 15 minutes
*Makes 24*
*Medium*

1 quantity butter cake (see page 96)
1 x 300 ml carton cream, whipped
sifted icing sugar for sprinkling

1. Preheat oven to 180°C. Line 24
muffin tins with paper cake cases.
2. Prepare cake batter. Spoon
mixture into paper cases. Bake for 15
minutes or until cooked when tested.
3. Cool on a wire rack. Cut a slice
from the top of each cake. Cut in half
to form wings. Top cakes with cream
and wings to make butterflies. Dust
with a little icing sugar.

## ANT FLOATER

*Preparation time*: 20 minutes
*Cooking time*: 15 minutes
*Makes 6 cups concentrate*
*Easy*

pulp of 12 large passionfruit
3 teaspoons tartaric acid
3 cups water
3 cups sugar

1. Put passionfruit pulp into a bowl,
stir in the tartaric acid. Heat water
and sugar together until boiling,
stirring until sugar dissolves. Then
boil for 10 minutes.
2. Add passionfruit pulp, cover and
leave until cold. Bottle and seal
securely. Serve diluted with iced water
or sparkling soda water.

*Ant Floaters*

*Porcupines*

*Bugs in Rugs*

## BUGS IN RUGS

*Preparation time:* 20 minutes
*Cooking time:* 15 minutes
*Makes 12*
*Easy*

12 cocktail frankfurters
3 slices bread
½ cup tomato sauce
¼ cup melted butter
2 tablespoons poppy seeds
toothpicks

1.  Preheat oven to 180°C. Lightly grease an oven tray. Pierce frankfurters all over with a fork.
2.  Spread a little tomato sauce on bread slices. Cut each slice of bread into quarters. Place a cocktail frankfurter diagonally on each quarter of bread. Bring up edges and secure with a toothpick. Brush liberally with melted butter and sprinkle with poppy seeds.
3.  Place on prepared oven tray, and bake for 10–15 minutes until bread is crisp and lightly brown. Remove from oven and serve hot or cold.

## SAMMY SNAKE

*Preparation time:* 30 minutes
*Cooking time:* nil
*Easy*

1 quantity of buttercream frosting
  (see page 96)
green food colouring
1 packet of 6 jam rollettes
assorted decorations: licorice straps,
  licorice allsorts (cut in diamond
  shapes), Smarties and assorted
  sweets
shredded coconut, tinted green

1.  Tint buttercream to desired shade of green with a little food colouring.
2.  Place jam rollettes on a tray or flat platter, joining together with some buttercream frosting to form a curved snake. Spread remaining buttercream over snake.
3.  Decorate using your favourite sweets. Sprinkle coconut around snake to represent grass. Chill until firm.

*Sammy Snake*

# Dinner Party

THIS PARTY makes a novel change from noisy Saturday afternoon bunfights. It is easy for working parents to arrange, as food can be prepared in advance and the table set the evening before. Parents or older siblings could enter into the spirit of things by serving the meal on silver trays, and acting the part of waiters to the sophisticated; draping a white cloth over one arm, and wearing white cotton gloves (available from most gardening shops, and not expensive). Invite guests to wear Formal Dress. They will enjoy dressing up in borrowed evening finery — long swishy skirts and flouncing feather boas, bow ties and jackets.

**Age group:** four to ten
**Venue:** home
**Number of guests:** up to 8

### Invitations
Make invitations from black card, decorated with silver glitter on the front. Use a silver pen or white crayon to invite guests to a Soirée at Six Thirty. Ask them to wear Formal Dress and remind them to R.S.V.P.

*Clockwise from left: Melon and Strawberry Cocktail, Number Cake, Tossed Salad, Chewy Chocolate Ice Cream Sundae, Spaghetti Bolognaise and Garlic Bread.*

### Decorations

Make the table setting as elegant as possible. Borrow a silver candelabra and use it as the centrepiece, with floral decorations around it and along the length of the table. Use tall plastic wine glasses with long stems to serve sparkling apple juice. Fold the table napkins into Lady Windermere Fans or other decorative shapes. Make small place cards for each guest. Write the menu out in flowing cursive writing, on a piece of card or mock parchment, and have it displayed on the table. Play soft background music and keep the lights low.

As each guest arrives, announce them formally. Serve them each a cocktail; fruit juice in long-stemmed plastic glasses, topped with a cherry, twisted slice of orange and tiny paper umbrella, with a novelty plastic swizzle stick. For extra impact, you could serve these in frosted glasses. To frost, dip the rim of each glass in egg white, then into caster sugar, and let the frosting harden in the fridge for ten or fifteen minutes before pouring the drinks.

As this is an evening party, guests will probably be ready for their meal soon after arriving. Plan to have the games after dinner, and have guests seated not later than half an hour after arriving.

### Food

*Entrée:* Melon and Strawberry Cocktail.

*Main course:* Spaghetti Bolognaise, served with tossed salad and garlic bread.

*Dessert:* The Number Cake, or Chewy Chocolate Ice-cream Sundaes.

*Melon and Strawberry Cocktail*

**Cake:** The Number Cake, made from choux pastry, could be served as a party cake, or could be served as an elegant dessert at the end of the meal. For a change from birthday candles, use thin tapers or sparklers instead. These will have extra impact if the cake is served in a darkened room.

## Games

After dinner, plan half an hour of quiet games such as *Hangman*, *Making words*, or *Hat making*. Have a *Memory test* or play *Mystery matchboxes*. More active games later could include *Bat the balloon*, *Wrap the mummy*, the *Chocolate game* or charades. Play *Hedgehogs*, *Find the bell ringer*, and *Balloon dress-ups*. A *Broomstick relay* is lots of fun, as is *Blindfold drawing*.

## Prizes and Party Favours

Inexpensive toy jewellery , novelty party hats, and cocktail accessories — tiny umbrellas, fancy swizzle sticks and small decorations (buy a packet of these and divide the contents into groups of three or four items, wrapped in cellophane). Party blowout tooters and whistles.

*Spaghetti Bolognaise*

## MELON AND STRAWBERRY COCKTAIL

*Preparation time:* 20 minutes plus
   1 hour chilling time
*Cooking time:* nil
*Serves 6*
*Easy*

½ rockmelon
½ honeydew melon
1 x 250 g punnet strawberries
1 tablespoon lemon juice
1 teaspoon sugar
fresh mint for garnish

1. Scrape seeds out of the centre of melons. Scoop out flesh using a melon baller, or peel and cut into 2 cm chunks. Wash and hull the strawberries and slice into halves. Toss fruit in sugar and lemon juice and chill for 1 hour.
2. Spoon fruit into six glass bowls or tall parfait-style glasses. Garnish with sprigs of mint and serve.

## SPAGHETTI BOLOGNAISE

*Preparation time:* 20 minutes
*Cooking time:* 1 hour
*Serves 6*
*Easy*

1 tablespoon vegetable oil
750 g minced beef
2 onions, finely chopped
1 clove garlic, crushed
1 x 425 g can of tomatoes
1 tablespoon lemon juice
2 tablespoons tomato paste
1 beef stock cube
½ teaspoon dried basil
½ teaspoon dried oregano
½ teaspoon sugar
3 tablespoons cold water
1 tablespoon plain flour
grated cheese for serving
385 g spaghetti
1 tablespoon oil (extra)

1. To make Bolognaise sauce: heat oil in a large pan. Add mince and cook in the oil until meat browns and separates into small pieces. Add garlic and onion, and fry a further 5 minutes.
2. Add tomatoes, tomato paste, lemon juice, stock cube, herbs and sugar. Stir to combine. Simmer for 40 minutes, stirring occasionally and breaking up tomato. Blend flour and water together to form a smooth paste. Add to meat mixture and return to boil, stirring constantly. Pour over cooked spaghetti and serve sprinkled with cheese.
3. To cook spaghetti: bring a large pan of water to the boil, add oil. Add spaghetti to rapidly boiling water, pushing spaghetti in gently until it is all submersed in the water. Stir once and boil rapidly for approximately 8 minutes or until firm but cooked through. Drain and serve immediately, topped with Bolognaise sauce.

## TOSSED SALAD

*Preparation time:* 15 minutes
*Cooking time:* nil
*Serves 6*
*Easy*

SALAD
1 lettuce, washed
2 tomatoes, washed
¼ cucumber, thickly peeled
2 stalks celery, washed
1 carrot, peeled
6 mushrooms

DRESSING
1 tablespoon oil
1 tablespoon white vinegar
3 tablespoons mayonnaise
1 tablespoon finely chopped fresh
    parsley

1.  Tear lettuce into bite-sized pieces
and place in a large salad bowl.
Remove core section from tomatoes
and cut into quarters. Slice cucumber
and celery. Cut carrot into thin sticks
and quarter mushrooms. Arrange
salad vegetables on top of lettuce and
toss lightly.
2.  To prepare dressing: combine all
ingredients in a screwtop jar and
shake well. Pour dressing over salad
just before serving.

*Tossed Salad*

*Chewy Chocolate Ice-cream Sundae*

## GARLIC BREAD

*Preparation time:* 15 minutes
*Cooking time:* 15 minutes
*Serves 6*
*Easy*

2 French bread sticks
200 g butter, softened
3 cloves garlic, crushed

1.  Preheat oven to 180°C. Slice
French sticks into 3 cm slices, cutting
all the way through. Arrange bread on
a large sheet of foil and re-form the
shape of the loaf.
2.  Cream together butter and garlic
until light and very soft. Spread bread
liberally on one side of each slice and
place back on foil. Push slices
together and wrap loaf tightly.
3.  Bake bread in oven for 10–15
minutes. Partially open foil packets
and serve.

## CHEWY CHOCOLATE ICE-CREAM SUNDAE

*Preparation time:* 15 minutes
*Cooking time:* 5 minutes
*Serves 6*
*Easy*

1 litre vanilla ice-cream
3 Mars Bars
½ cup cream
2 Milky Ways
1 Flake, crumbled
1 Scorched Peanut Bar, broken into
    small pieces
6 ice-cream wafers

1. Roughly chop Mars Bars in small pieces and place in a heatproof bowl with cream. Heat over simmering water until melted. Cool slightly. Slice Milky Ways into 1 cm slices.
2. Place a small scoop of ice-cream into each of six parfait glasses. Divide half the Mars Bar mixture, Milky Way pieces and Scorched Peanut Bar between the glasses. Top each serving with another scoop of ice-cream then top with remaining Mars mixture, Milky Ways and Scorched Peanut Bars. Sprinkle with crumbled Flake and insert an ice-cream wafer on top of each glass. Serve immediately.

NOTE
Chocolate bars with flavoured creamy fillings and peanut brittle can be substituted for Mars Bars, Milky Ways and Scorched Peanut Bars.

*Number Cake*

## NUMBER CAKE

*Preparation time:* 1 hour
*Cooking time:* 1 hour
*Medium*

CAKE
1 cup water
60 g butter, cut into small pieces
1 cup plain flour
1 teaspoon sugar
3 eggs

TOPPING
500 ml cream
1 tablespoon sugar
1 teaspoon vanilla essence
2 cups glacé icing (see page 96) or
    150 g melted chocolate
assorted sweets for decoration

1. Preheat oven to 210°C. Grease an oven tray and mark on it, as a large number, the child's age. Heat water and butter in a pan and bring to the boil. Sift flour and sugar together and add all at once to boiling butter and water mixture. Remove from heat and beat well until no lumps remain and mixture is thick. Return to low heat and stir until mixture leaves the sides of the pan. Remove from heat and cool.
2. Beat eggs lightly. Add a little at a time to flour mixture, beating well after each addition. When all the egg has been added, the mixture should be thick and glossy.
3. Spoon or pipe batter onto prepared tray in the shape of the number required. Bake for 20 minutes or until puffed. Reduce heat to 180°C and cook for a further 30–40 minutes or until golden, and crisp to touch. Remove from oven and cool on a wire rack.
4. To prepare topping: whip cream with sugar and vanilla until soft peaks form. Slit cake in half horizontally, fill with cream and replace top.
5. Place filled cake on a wire rack with a clean oven tray underneath. Warm icing or melt chocolate and pour immediately over the cake, allowing excess to drip off. If needed, the excess may be re-melted and poured over again. Before icing or chocolate cools, top with an assortment of sweets and add candles.

# United Nations Party

THE UNITED NATIONS party allows children a special opportunity to talk about the origins of their own families, and is fun for older children. Asking guests to come dressed in the national dress of a member of their family, or of their favourite country, will lead to a very colourful and interesting variety of dress. Many will be able to borrow items of national dress — Dutch clogs or lace caps, saris, kimonos, happy coats — and will be able to augment these with appropriate extras from their own wardrobes; black trousers with happy coats, for example.

**Age group:** seven to eleven
**Venue:** home
**Number of guests:** up to 12

### Invitations
Make paper fans and write the invitations on those, or make small strings of flags, with the front coloured in, and the different parts of the invitation — time, place, address and so on — written on the back of each flag. Thread these together with cotton. Invite each guest to make their chosen country's national flag on a big sheet of paper, and to bring that to the party. Also ask each guest to make and bring their own 'passport', showing their country of origin, a self-portrait, and a description of themselves.

### Decorations
Make flags and bunting from coloured paper or butcher's paper, and string these up about the party room. You may also be able to borrow bunting from your local supermarket or garage — supermarket bunting often shows world flags.

Display a globe or map of the world near the door. As each guest arrives, ask them to mark their chosen country with a yellow flag or sticker. Have a clothesline and pegs ready to hang each guest's national flag. Cut a

potato-print stamp, or find a pictorial rubber stamp, and stamp their 'passports'.

A local travel agency may lend you posters of exotic faraway places for displaying on the walls, or you could collect suitable pictures from coloured magazines and pin those up. Hang travel brochures on pieces of string from the ceiling.

### Food
Serve a multi-national menu — Hawaiian Delights, Italian Fruit and Chocolate Cassata, Indonesian Satay with Peanut Sauce, Middle Eastern Hummus, Chinese Spring Rolls, mini Italian Pizzas and Island Coolers.

**Cake:** for an international flavour make an Australia cake.

### Games

As an ice-breaker, ask all the guests to sit in a circle. Taking turns, each child stands, shows his or her national dress, and talks about it and the country from which it comes. Encourage them by asking questions about what language is spoken there, what the capital city is, and why they have chosen it.

Play *Making words*, using the names of countries and cities as the starting point.

Play *Musical sets*, *Trains and stations*, *Taste and guess*, and *Chopsticks and marbles*. Have a doughnut eating race and play *Guess in the dark*. Play *Postman's holiday*, using countries and capital cities instead of town or street names.

### Prizes and Party Favours

Incense sticks, paper fans, packets of origami paper, pencil sharpeners made like world globes, or extra-long pencils tipped with small flags.

---

*Clockwise from left: Indonesian Satay with Peanut Sauce, Australia Cake, Island Coolers, Mini Italian Pizzas, Middle Eastern Hummus, Hawaiian Delights, Italian Fruit and Chocolate Cassata , Chinese Spring Rolls.*

*Indonesian Satay with Peanut Sauce*

1. Slice bread into 10 thick slices. Spread with butter, and top with slices of ham.
2. Halve each slice of pineapple horizontally and place on top of ham. Top with cheese.
3. Place under a preheated griller until cheese melts and browns. Cut into fingers to serve.

HINT
As a variation, make these delicious snacks on small rounds of pita bread instead of crusty bread.

*Chinese Spring Rolls*

## CHINESE SPRING ROLLS

*Preparation time:* 35 minutes
*Cooking time:* 30 minutes
*Makes 12*
*Medium*

250 g chicken breasts, skinned and finely chopped
1 tablespoon oil
6 shallots, finely sliced
200 g fresh bean sprouts
3 mushrooms, finely chopped
1 tablespoon chicken stock
1 tablespoon soy sauce
2 teaspoons cornflour mixed with 1 tablespoon cold water
10–12 spring-roll wrappers (or use filo pastry sheets cut into 20 cm squares)

1. Preheat oven to 200°C. Add chicken and oil to a preheated wok or pan. Stir-fry for 2–3 minutes. Add shallots, bean sprouts and mushrooms. Stir-fry for 2 minutes.
2. Mix together chicken stock, soy sauce and blended cornflour. Add to wok, stirring until sauce thickens. Allow mixture to cool. Drain off excess liquid.
3. Divide mixture into 12 portions. Place one portion in the centre of a spring-roll wrapper. Fold over sides. Roll up into a parcel and seal with a little water. Bake all parcels for 30 minutes until golden brown, or deep-fry in hot oil for 3–5 minutes and drain on absorbent paper. Serve hot.

## HAWAIIAN DELIGHTS

*Preparation time:* 20 minutes
*Cooking time:* 5 minutes
*Serves 10*
*Easy*

1 loaf crusty bread
butter for spreading
10 slices sandwich ham
5 slices canned pineapple
10 slices processed or cheddar cheese

*Hawaiian Delights*

## INDONESIAN SATAY WITH PEANUT SAUCE

*Preparation time:* 45 minutes plus
  overnight marinating time
*Cooking time:* 15 minutes
*Makes 50*
*Easy*

SATAY
1.5 kg lean pork or chicken
3 onions, chopped
1 cup soy sauce
3 cloves garlic
¾ cup white vinegar
juice 2 lemons
2 teaspoons turmeric
1 teaspoon cumin
ground black pepper
skewers

PEANUT SAUCE
2 tablespoons oil
2 onions, finely chopped
2 cloves garlic, crushed
1 cup coconut cream
juice 1 lemon
2 tablespoons soy sauce
2 tablespoons tomato sauce
2 teaspoons chilli sauce (optional)
½ cup crunchy peanut butter

1.  Cut meat into bite-sized cubes.
Place in a large bowl. Place remaining
satay ingredients in a food processor
or blender and process to a purée.
Pour purée over meat and toss well to
coat cubes thoroughly. Cover and
refrigerate overnight to marinate.
2.  Thread meat onto skewers. Grill or
barbecue for 5–10 minutes, turning
frequently.
3.  To prepare peanut sauce: heat oil
in a large pan. Sauté onions and
garlic until onions are soft. Add all
remaining ingredients except peanut
butter. Bring to the boil, stirring
constantly. Reduce heat and simmer
for 3 minutes. Stir in peanut butter.
Spoon sauce over satays. Serve warm
or cool, with any remaining sauce in
a small bowl as an accompaniment.

HINT
If using wooden skewers, soak them
in cold water for at least 20 minutes
before threading the meat onto them.
This will prevent them from burning
when grilled.

*Italian Fruit and Chocolate Cassata*

## ITALIAN FRUIT AND CHOCOLATE CASSATA

*Preparation time:* 20 minutes plus
  freezing time
*Cooking time:* nil
*Serves 15*

2 litres vanilla ice-cream (see note)
30 g white chocolate, roughly chopped
60 g dark chocolate, roughly chopped
1½ cups walnuts, roughly chopped
1½ cups slivered almonds
1½ cups raisins
1 cup red cherries, halved
1 x 100 g pkt marshmallows, halved
½ cup strawberry flavouring
extra strawberry flavouring

1.  Lightly brush a 3 litre pudding
basin with oil. Invert on a rack to
drain away excess.
2.  Soften ice-cream slightly and
transfer to a large chilled bowl. Add
white and dark chocolate, nuts,
raisins, cherries, marshmallows and
strawberry flavouring. Mix through
ice-cream until only just combined.
Spoon into prepared pudding basin
and return to freezer to become firm.
3.  To serve: invert pudding basin
onto a serving plate, and cover with a
warm cloth for 1 minute. Gently shake
plate and bowl together until ice-
cream is released. Drizzle a little
strawberry flavouring over ice-cream.

NOTE
Use a good quality ice-cream for this
recipe. The lesser quality ice-creams
melt and lose volume very quickly on
softening.

*Mini Italian Pizzas*

*Middle Eastern Hummus*

## MIDDLE EASTERN HUMMUS

*Preparation time:* 20 minutes plus
    overnight soaking time
*Cooking time:* 1 hour
*Makes about 4 cups*
*Easy*

1½ cups chick peas
1 cup lemon juice
⅓ cup water
2 tablespoons white vinegar
3 cloves garlic, chopped
1 cup tahini paste
2 tablespoons olive oil
extra olive oil to serve
mild paprika
10 pita breads

1.  Place chick peas in a large pan,
cover with hot water and leave to soak
overnight.

2.  Drain and return to saucepan.
Cover with hot water again. Bring to
the boil and cook for about 1 hour or
until soft.
3.  Drain. Place chick peas in a food
processor or blender. Process to a
purée with lemon juice and water.
Add vinegar, garlic, tahini and olive
oil. Process again to a creamy paste.
Adjust seasoning. Add more lemon
juice, if required. Drizzle a little olive
oil over the top and sprinkle with
paprika. Serve accompanied with pita
bread cut into quarters.

HINT
Tahini paste is a thick paste made
from a base of crushed sesame seeds
with a little water, salt and lemon
juice. The consistency is similar to
peanut butter. It is readily available at
large supermarkets or delicatessens.

## ISLAND COOLER

*Preparation time:* 5 minutes
*Cooking time:* nil
*Serves 8*
*Easy*

1 x 850 ml can pineapple juice
¼ cup lemon juice
½ cup coconut milk
1 x 1 litre bottle lemonade
Ice cubes
Pineapple slices for serving

1.  Mix together juices and coconut
milk. Transfer to a large jug. Chill
thoroughly.
2.  Just before serving add lemonade.
Garnish with a few ice-cubes and a
slice of pineapple.

*Island Cooler*

## MINI ITALIAN PIZZAS

*Preparation time:* 35 minutes
*Cooking time:* 20 minutes
*Makes 8*
*Easy*

2 sheets frozen shortcrust pastry,
    thawed
¼ cup tomato sauce
2 slices ham, chopped
1 x 225 g tin sliced pineapple, drained
    and chopped
1 stick cabanossi or other sausage,
    sliced thinly
4 mushrooms, chopped
2 cups shredded cheese

1.  Preheat oven to 180°C. Cut circles
of pastry using a large scone or biscuit
cutter. Alternatively, cut each sheet
of pastry into four circles, using a
sharp knife and a glass. Spread each
circle with tomato sauce. Top with
ham, pineapple, cabanossi slices and
mushrooms. Sprinkle with cheese.
2.  Place on an ungreased baking
tray. Bake for 15–20 minutes or until
pastry is crisp and cheese has melted.
Serve hot from the oven.

HINT
Thinly sliced rings of onion can be
added for a tasty variation.

*Australia Cake*

## AUSTRALIA CAKE

*Preparation time:* 45 minutes
*Cooking time:* 25 minutes
*Easy*

2 x 350 g packets cake mix or
    2 quantities butter cake batter
    (see page 96)
½ quantity buttercream frosting
    (see page 96)
500 g icing sugar
¼ cup cocoa
½ cup boiling water
1 teaspoon butter
250 g desiccated coconut
1 small Australian flag and candles for
    decoration

1.  Preheat oven to 180°C. Grease
and line two 22 x 32 cm Swiss roll tins
with greaseproof paper and grease
again. Make cakes according to
directions on the packet or following

recipe. Divide mixture between
prepared tins and bake for 20–25
minutes or until cooked when tested.
Cool in tins for 5 minutes before
turning out onto a wire rack to cool
completely.
2.  Spread one cake with frosting and
place other cake on top. Mark shape
of Australia on cake, using diagram as
a guide. Use a sharp knife to cut out
the shape.
3.  Sift together icing sugar and
cocoa. Stir in boiling water and
butter. Blend until smooth, with the
consistency of cream. Add a little
extra water if necessary. Place cake
on a rack over a clean tray. Drizzle
chocolate mixture over cake and allow
it to flood over the sides, ensuring
cake is completely covered with
chocolate. Sprinkle liberally with
desiccated coconut. Stand 30 minutes
until icing sets.

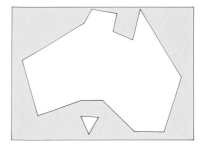

4.  Lift cake onto a large board.
Decorate with an Australian flag and
candles.

HINT
To adapt the shape of this cake to
that of another country, simply trace
the required map outline from a large
atlas and use the tracing as a cutting
guide. Decorate with appropriate
flags.

# SportsParty

W HAT TO WEAR poses no problem at all for this party theme, which is great fun for older children. Guests can dress in their own sports gear, or be invited to dress as their favourite sports heroes. They will have their own sports outfits to use, or could raid the wardrobes of friends and neighbours.

Before the party, set up a mini-golf course in your garden or garage. Pieces of cardboard make good slopes, loose bricks create low side walls, and tunnels can be constructed from cardboard boxes cut in half, or shoe boxes. Bottle sleeves made from paper, through which the ball must be putted, add a challenge. Have a golf club (borrowed from neighbours if necessary) for each player, and play with used golf balls.

Set up a ping-pong table in the carport. Invest in an inexpensive ping-pong set (table net, two or four bats and ping-pong balls) if you don't already have one. Ping-pong is a perennial favourite and the investment will be a popular one in the long term.

**Age group:** eight to eleven
**Venue:** home
**Number of guests:** up to 10

### Invitations
Cut out cardboard cricket balls from folded red card, or cut single ping-pong bat shapes and write the invitations on those. Invite the team to join you for a sports tournament, and give kick-off time.

### Decorations
Borrow all the sports equipment you can from friends. Use it to give a sporty flavour to the party room. Hang crossed hockey sticks, tennis racquets or cricket bats on the wall, and add cricket scarves, hats, football boots and ice-skates. Pin up a rugby jersey or two. If you can, borrow victors' shields and cups from the local sports club and display these as well, or paint mock shields on cardboard and hang those up. Big cheerleaders' pom-poms are easy to make, using strips of coloured crêpe paper taped onto lengths of bamboo.

### Food
Serve Bats and Balls, Soccer Balls, Soft Pitch, Sportstar Stamina, Throw in the Bat, and Players' Meat Pies. Add a big bowl of orange wedges for refreshment at half-time.

**Cake:** score a point with the Racquet cake.

### Games
Play ping-pong or mini-golf. Arrange a *Tug of war*, a *Blow the balloon* race and a game of balloon tennis, where balloons are batted from team to team instead of tennis balls. Play *Bat the balloon*; bob for apples, and have a *Doughnut eating race*.

Or play *Bean bag hockey*. The

equipment needed for this is simple — a small beanbag, two chairs, and two newspapers, each rolled up tightly and tied with string to form a stick.

Divide the children into two teams, and line them up on opposite sides of the room, facing each other. Give each member of one team a number, from left to right, and number the other team with the same numbers from right to left. The teams will then face each other like this:

$$1 \quad 2 \quad 3 \quad 4 \quad 5$$
$$5 \quad 4 \quad 3 \quad 2 \quad 1$$

In the centre of the floor, place the newspaper sticks and the beanbag. Place a chair against each far wall, in the middle. Each chair represents a goal for one team.

The referee must call out one of the team numbers. At the call, the two team members of that number have to run forward, pick up a newspaper stick, and try to hit the beanbag into goal between their team's chair legs; then sticks have to be replaced in the centre. The referee can keep the pace very fast. The team with the most

goals at the end of the allotted time, or when the whistle goes, wins.

**Prizes and Party Favours**
Tennis and ping-pong balls, inexpensive sun visors, small bottles of coloured zinc to protect noses from sunburn, aniseed balls.

---

*Clockwise from left: Sportstar Stamina, Players' Meat Pie, Throw in the Bat, Bats and Balls, Soccer Balls and Soft Pitch*

*Bats and Balls*

in a heatproof bowl over simmering water, and stir over a low heat until melted. Spread the underside of half the flat biscuits with a little chocolate marshmallow mixture.

4. Decorate the top of the remaining biscuits with glacé icing tinted several colours. Place in the oven (180°C) for 5 minutes to set. Remove from oven and cool slightly, prior to joining biscuit halves. Decorate balls with glacé icing and allow to set on a wire rack.

## SPORTSTAR STAMINA

*Preparation time*: 25 minutes plus
   chilling time
*Cooking time*: 20 minutes
*Makes 8 cups*
*Easy*

**4 large lemons**
**1½ cups sugar**
**2 cups water**
**1 cup lemon juice**
**1 litre extra cold water**
**lemon slices for serving**

1. Peel rind from lemons as thinly as possible. Put in a pan with sugar and 2 cups water. Simmer for 20 minutes. Strain and set aside until cold.
2. Stir lemon juice and 1 litre water into the cold syrup and chill well. Serve in tall tumblers over crushed ice and top each with a lemon slice.

## BATS AND BALLS

*Preparation time*: 1 hour plus
   20 minutes chilling time
*Cooking time*: 10 minutes per batch
*Makes about 50*
*Easy*

**125 g butter**
**½ cup sugar**
**1 egg**
**½ teaspoon cinnamon**
**1½ cups plain flour**
**2 tablespoons cornflour**
**100 g marshmallows**
**100 g chocolate**
**2 x 10 cm lengths licorice**
**1 cup glacé icing (see page 96)**
**food colouring**

1. Preheat oven to 220°C and grease an oven tray and a shallow muffin tray. Cream butter and sugar together until pale, light and fluffy. Beat in egg until mixture is smooth and creamy. Sift together cinnamon, plain flour and cornflour. Add to butter mixture, and mix well with a flat-bladed knife. Form mixture into a ball. Chill covered in the refrigerator for 20 minutes.

2. On a lightly floured board roll out two-thirds of the dough to 5 mm thick. Cut dough into bat and racquet shapes of similar size. Arrange on prepared tray and bake for 8–10 minutes or until biscuits are a pale golden brown. Remove from oven and cool on tray. Shape remaining dough into footballs, soccer balls and cricket balls. Bake these for 5–10 minutes in shallow muffin containers to prevent them rolling everywhere. Remove from oven and cool on tray.

3. Place marshmallows and chocolate

*Sportstar Stamina*

## SOFT PITCH

*Preparation time:* 5 minutes
*Cooking time:* nil
*Makes 6*
*Easy*

⅓ cup crunchy peanut butter
½ cup plain yoghurt
1 tablespoon chopped chives or shallots
1 tablespoon peanut or vegetable oil
1 teaspoon soy sauce or soy manis
fresh vegetables for serving

1. Beat together peanut butter and yoghurt. Add remaining ingredients except vegetables, and stir well.
2. Spoon into four small bowls or ramekins and place on serving plates. Surround with strips and slices of raw vegetables.

NOTE
Soy Manis is an Indonesian-style soy sauce which has a delicious, slightly sweet, soy flavour.

*Soft Pitch*

*Soccer Balls*

## SOCCER BALLS

*Preparation time:* 30 minutes
*Cooking time:* nil
*Makes 40*
*Easy*

1 cup very finely chopped dried
  apricots
1 cup desiccated coconut
½ cup sweetened condensed milk
extra desiccated coconut

1. In a bowl combine apricots, coconut and condensed milk, mixing very thoroughly.
2. Take 2 teaspoons of mixture and form into a small ball. Repeat with remaining mixture. Toss balls in extra desiccated coconut. Place in the refrigerator and chill well.

NOTE
These can be made a week ahead and stored in an airtight container in the refrigerator.

HINT
Chopping dried fruit is easy if you use sharp scissors dipped in boiling water.

*Throw in the Bat*

*Players' Meat Pie*

## THROW IN THE BAT

*Preparation time:* 20 minutes
*Cooking time:* 20 minutes
*Makes 12*
*Easy*

½ cup plain flour
1 egg
¼ cup milk
½ cup water
12 chipolata sausages or cocktail
   frankfurters
tomato sauce or baked beans to serve

1. Preheat oven to 210°C. Lightly oil 12 small muffin tins.
2. Sift flour into a bowl. Whisk together egg, milk and water, and gradually add to flour. Whisk until batter is smooth.
3. Place a sausage in each prepared muffin cup. Bake for 5 minutes. Whisk batter again and quickly pour around sausages in cups. Bake 10–15 minutes more until well risen and browned. Serve hot with tomato sauce or baked beans.

## PLAYERS' MEAT PIE

*Preparation time:* 35 minutes
*Cooking time:* 1½ hours
*Makes 1*
*Medium*

PIE BASE
1 sheet frozen ready-rolled shortcrust
   pastry

PIE TOP
1 sheet frozen ready-rolled puff pastry

FILLING
1 tablespoon oil
30 g butter
750 g blade steak, trimmed and cubed
2 cups beef stock
pinch pepper
2 tablespoons cornflour
1 cup water
1 tablespoon worcestershire sauce

1. Preheat oven to 200°C. Line the base of a 23 cm pie plate with pastry. Trim edges. Rest in the refrigerator until required.
2. To prepare filling: heat oil and butter in a large frypan. Add meat in

batches and brown well. Drain off excess fat. Return meat to pan with stock and pepper to taste. Simmer, covered, for 40 minutes or until meat is tender.
3. Blend cornflour with a little water to form a smooth paste. Blend in remaining water and worcestershire sauce. Add to meat and return to the boil, stirring until thickened. Simmer 5 minutes, remove from heat and cool.
4. Fill pie case with meat. Wet pastry edges with a little water. Top with puff pastry sheet. Trim edges and press together to seal. Make a cut in the centre of pastry top with a sharp knife. Brush top with milk and bake for 35–40 minutes or until puffed and golden.

NOTE
This may be made into individual party pies by lining muffin tins with shortcrust pastry. Fill with meat and top with rounds of puff pastry. Bake for 10–15 minutes or until golden brown.

## BADMINTON RACQUET CAKE

*Preparation time:* 1¼ hours
*Cooking time:* 40 minutes
*Medium*

2 x 350 g packets cake mix or
   2 quantities butter cake batter
   (see page 96)
1 quantity butter icing (see page 96)
3 tablespoons cocoa
2 tablespoons hot water
Smarties

1. Preheat oven to 180°C. Grease and line both a 20 cm round cake tin and a 20 cm square cake tin. Make the cakes according to the directions on the packet or following recipe. Divide mixture between prepared tins and bake for 35–40 minutes or until cooked. Cool.

2. Dissolve cocoa in hot water and cool. Mix cocoa with half the butter icing, leaving remaining butter icing plain. Reserve ½ cup plain butter icing for decoration.

3. Trim the sides of the round cake to give an oval shape (see diagram 1). Cut the square cake vertically in three, to give two pieces each 8 cm wide and one narrower piece (see diagram). The remaining piece is not used so you could use it in another recipe.

4. Join the small ends of the two rectangular pieces of cake together with a little icing. Cover completely with plain butter icing. This forms the handle of the racquet.

5. Place the handle on a cake board, leaving enough room for the head of the racquet. Using the chocolate icing, ice the top of the oval cake smoothly, leaving an uniced 1.5 cm rim around the outside.

Using the plain icing, ice the sides of the cake and the 1.5 cm rim, covering the edges of chocolate icing slightly so that the two colours join together evenly.

6. Fill a piping bag with the reserved ½ cup of plain icing. Pipe lines over the chocolate icing to represent the strings on the racquet (see diagram 3). Place a row of Smarties around the outer edge of the cake where the chocolate icing and the plain butter icing meet (see diagram 4).

7. Transfer the head of the racquet to the cake board and join it to the handle with a little icing. Use Smarties around the base of the handle to represent a hand grip. Using a star nozzle, pipe a row of rosettes around the base of the cake.

HINT
Instead of using Smarties to decorate the cake, pipe rosettes in their place. For rosettes, make an extra ½ quantity of butter icing and colour it part red, part yellow.

*Badminton Racquet Cake*

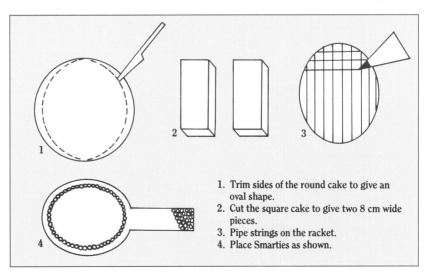

1. Trim sides of the round cake to give an oval shape.
2. Cut the square cake to give two 8 cm wide pieces.
3. Pipe strings on the racket.
4. Place Smarties as shown.

# DiscoParty

T HIS IS POPULAR with older children, who enjoy it all the more
if it is held at night rather than in the afternoon. If you have
a garage, basement or family room that can be cleared and used
strictly for party purposes, so much the better. Furnishings in the
party room are minimal, to allow space for dancing — heaps of
scatter cushions are usually sufficient. Guests usually find no
problem in assembling an appropriate wardrobe, often borrowed
from older brothers or sisters. Neighbours might appreciate a word
of warning before the event.

**Age group:** ten to twelve
**Venue:** home
**Number of guests:** up to 12

### Invitations
Cut up popular teenage or motorbike
magazines and make a collage of
pictures on the front of each
invitation. Alternatively, cut card into
hamburger-shaped invitations and
have the host illustrate the front of
each card. Invite the gang over to a
wild rage.

### Decorations
Cover the table with a shiny black or
red vinyl tablecloth and use red paper
serviettes with glossy coloured paper
plates and mugs. Tie bunches of
brightly-coloured balloons to lengths
of thin stick, wind red crêpe paper
round the sticks, and prop these on
the table and on window ledges.
Invest in a few differently coloured
light bulbs, and exchange these for
the plain ones in your light fittings; or
hang up a string of coloured lights.

### Food
Serve Mini Burgers, Shoe String
Fries, Chilli Con Carne, Guacamole
and Corn Chips, American Hot Dogs,
Pecan Chocolate Brownies, Apple Pie
and Disco Delight Biscuits.

**Cake:** tune in with the Ghetto Blaster.

### Games
Turn the room into a disco and have
the host be responsible for equipment
and sound. Dancing will be the main
feature of the party, but you could
suggest a few alternatives to keep
things moving; dancing competitions,
for example, or a variation of *Hop and
pop*, during which guests must keep
dancing whilst trying to pop each
other's balloons.

For a complete change of pace,
suggest a break for *Murder in the
dark*, *Guess in the dark* or *Charades*.

### Prizes and Party Favours
Fake fingernail sets, inexpensive
earrings or other jewellery,
sunglasses, badges and novelty straws.

## SHOE STRING FRIES

*Preparation time:* 20 minutes
*Cooking time:* 30 minutes
*Serves 10*
*Medium*

2 kg large potatoes, thinly peeled
vegetable oil for deep-frying

1. Wash and thoroughly dry potatoes. Cut lengthways into fine shoestring lengths. Pat potatoes dry with absorbent paper.

2. Half-fill a pan or deep-fryer with oil. Heat slowly until the surface of the oil appears to move.

3. Place shoestring potatoes, a few at a time, into a wire basket and lower into hot oil. Fry for a few minutes until pale golden. Drain on absorbent paper. Continue with remaining shoestrings until all are parcooked.

4. When ready to serve, reheat oil. Cook chips again in batches, until crisp and golden. Drain well on absorbent paper. Serve with mini burgers (see recipe, page 90).

*Clockwise from left: Pecan Chocolate Brownies, Shoestring Fries, American Hot Dogs, Chilli Con Carne, Apple Pie, Guacamole and Corn Chips, Disco Delights, and Mini Burgers.*

*Pecan Chocolate Brownies*

3. In a mixing bowl, beat butter and vanilla, gradually adding sugar until mixture is light and fluffy. Beat in eggs, one at a time, then beat in chocolate until blended. Sift in flour and stir until combined. Fold in pecans.

4. Spread mixture evenly into prepared tin. Bake for 25–30 minutes or until cooked through and a crust forms on the surface. Cool slightly and cut into squares. Cool completely and remove from tin. To serve, dust top with icing sugar.

*Guacamole and Corn Chips*

## GUACAMOLE AND CORN CHIPS

*Preparation time:* 10 minutes
*Cooking time:* nil
*Serves 10*
*Easy*

2 ripe avocados
juice of 1 lemon
1 clove garlic, crushed
½ onion, finely grated
2 tomatoes, finely chopped
½ cup sour cream
few drops of tabasco sauce
100 g corn chips for serving

1. Mash avocados until smooth. Blend in lemon juice, garlic, onion, tomatoes, sour cream and sauce. Spoon into dip bowls and serve with corn chips.

## PECAN CHOCOLATE BROWNIES

*Preparation time:* 35 minutes
*Cooking time:* 35 minutes
*Makes 12*
*Easy*

60 g dark cooking chocolate
125 g butter
½ teaspoon vanilla essence
1 cup sugar
2 eggs
1 cup plain flour
¾ cup chopped pecans
sifted icing sugar to garnish (optional)

1. Preheat oven to 180°C and grease a 20 cm square cake tin.
2. Melt chocolate in a heatproof bowl over simmering water. Set aside to cool.

## APPLE PIE

*Preparation time:* 45 minutes plus
  chilling time
*Cooking time:* 45 minutes
*Makes 1*
*Medium*

PASTRY
1½ cups wholemeal flour
1½ cups plain flour
1 teaspoon mixed spice
100g butter
3–4 tablespoons cold water

FILLING
6 green apples, cored
¼ cup sultanas
4 tablespoons sugar
extra sugar

1. Preheat oven to 180°C and grease a 23 cm pie dish.
2. To prepare pastry: sift flours and mixed spice into a bowl. Return bran from sifter to bowl. Mix well to combine. Rub butter into flour using fingertips until mixture resembles fine

breadcrumbs. Add water gradually to make a soft dough. Wrap in plastic or waxed paper. Chill in refrigerator for 20 minutes.

3.  Roll out two-thirds of the pastry on a lightly floured surface or between two sheets of plastic wrap until pastry is 5 mm thick. Line prepared pie dish with pastry, trimming off excess. Roll out remaining pastry to cover pie. Set aside.

4.  To prepare filling: cut apples into thin slices. Layer in pie dish. Sprinkle each layer of apples with sultanas and sugar. Cover with remaining pastry and seal edges with water. Brush pastry with water and sprinkle with sugar. Cover with rolled pastry. Bake for 45 minutes or until apples are tender and pastry is golden brown.

## DISCO DELIGHT BISCUITS

*Preparation time:* 30 minutes plus
    30 minutes chilling time
*Cooking time:* 15 minutes
*Makes 16*
*Easy*

125 g butter
½ cup sugar
½ teaspoon vanilla essence
1 egg
1 cup plain flour
½ cup cornflour
½ cup self-raising flour
mock cream or jam
small red, green, yellow or orange
    unsugared jujubes

1.  Beat together butter, sugar and vanilla essence until creamy. Add egg and beat well. Sift flours into mixture and work in to form a firm dough. Wrap and chill about 20 minutes.

2.  Preheat oven to 180°C and grease an oven tray. Roll out into a sheet about 30 x 30 cm. Cut into strips 8 x 4 cm. Using a plain icing pipe or an essence bottle top, cut three holes in half the biscuits, leaving the rest whole.

3.  Arrange on prepared tray and bake for 15 minutes, or until lightly browned. When cold, join together in pairs with mock cream or jam, plain biscuit underneath. Put jujubes in each round to represent lights — red, yellow or orange and green.

*Disco Delight Biscuits*

## AMERICAN HOT DOGS

*Preparation time:* 15 minutes
*Cooking time:* 10 minutes
*Serves 10*
*Easy*

10 frankfurters
10 long hot dog rolls
American-style mustard (see note)
tomato sauce

1.  Arrange frankfurters on a griller tray and pierce skin with a fork. Place under grill and cook, turning regularly for 10 minutes or until the frankfurters are cooked and skin appears blistered.

2.  Split rolls lengthways without cutting all the way through. Spread lightly with a little mustard. Place each frankfurter in a roll and top with tomato sauce. Serve hot.

NOTE
American-style mustard is very mild. It may be omitted if you prefer.

*American Hot Dogs*

*Mini Burgers*

## CHILLI CON CARNE

*Preparation time:* 20 minutes
*Cooking time:* 55 minutes
*Serves 10*
*Easy*

2 tablespoons oil
1 kg minced beef
4 onions, chopped
1 clove garlic, crushed
1 teaspoon Mexican-style chilli powder
2 teaspoons paprika
1 teaspoon ground cumin
½ teaspoon ground coriander
1 x 800 g can peeled tomatoes
2 tablespoons tomato paste
1 beef stock cube, crumbled
1 x 750 g can red kidney beans
2 tablespoons cornflour blended with
    4 tablespoons water
bread rolls or steamed rice

*Chilli Con Carne*

## MINI BURGERS

*Preparation time:* 40 minutes
*Cooking time:* 10 minutes
*Serves 10*
*Easy*

1 teaspoon vegetable oil
1 onion, finely diced
500 g minced beef
1 stick French bread or 10 small
    dinner rolls
butter
4 leaves lettuce, finely shredded
2 tomatoes, sliced thinly
1 carrot, finely grated
125 g cheese, finely shredded
tomato sauce

1.  Heat oil in a pan and fry onion until soft. Combine with beef in a bowl. Divide mixture into 10 portions. Using wet hands, shape meat into flat patties a little larger than the diameter of the French bread or dinner rolls.

2.  Place meat patties under a hot grill and cook 3–5 minutes each side, turning once until patties are browned and cooked on both sides. Slice French bread thinly into 20 slices or split dinner rolls in half. Toast bread or rolls lightly on one side. Spread with butter.

3.  To serve: place each meat patty on bread and top with lettuce, tomato, carrot and cheese. Top with tomato sauce and bread. Insert a toothpick through the centre of the hamburger to hold it together.

HINT
Meat patties may be cooked in advance and reheated in the microwave at serving time, before assembling hamburgers; or the meat patties can be cooked in the oven at 200°C for 10–15 minutes or until cooked through.

1.  Heat oil in a large pan and add mince, a little at a time. Cook until mince browns and separates into small pieces. Add onions, garlic and spices and cook 5 minutes. Add tomatoes, tomato paste and stock cube. Return to the boil, then reduce heat and simmer for 45–50 minutes.
2.  Add undrained kidney beans, stir well and reheat. Add cornflour mixture a little at a time until mixture thickens. Return to the boil. Serve hot with fresh bread rolls or bowls of steamed rice.

*for cake
see blue pages, at the*
*props.* *front* *like*
*cake* *mike*
DISCO PARTY

## GHETTO BLASTER

*Preparation time:* 1½ hours
*Cooking time:* 50 minutes
*Advanced*

2 x 350 g packets cake mix or
    2 quantities butter cake batter (see
    recipe page 96)
2 x 450 g packets soft white icing
orange food colouring
¾ cup seedless jam, warmed
black food colouring
1 cup icing sugar
2–3 tablespoons water
2 licorice allsorts
1 chocolate bar e.g. Flake

1.  Preheat oven to 180°C. Grease
and line two 20 cm square cake tins.
Make the cakes according to the
directions on the packet or following
recipe. Divide the mixture between
prepared tins and bake for 40–50
minutes or until cooked. Cool.
2.  Cut one cake in half vertically to
form the speakers. Roll the two
packets of soft white icing together
and colour orange. Cut off one-fifth of
the icing and set it aside for the
markings and finishing touches.
Divide the remaining icing in half and
cut one half in half again.
3.  Roll out the larger piece of icing
until it is large enough to cover the
top and sides of the uncut cake with
about 1 cm extra on each side. Brush
the cake with warm jam and using a
rolling pin, roll the prepared icing
over the cake. Turn the cake over and
brush the edge of the underside with
warm jam. Bring the excess icing over
and press into the jam. Set the cake
upright (see diagrams 1 and 2).
Repeat this process with the two
smaller pieces of icing, covering the
two pieces of cake for speakers.
4.  Roll out the reserved small piece
(one-fifth) of soft icing to about
16 x 22 cm. From it, cut two 4 cm
circles to form round speakers, and
two rectangles about 4 x 7 cm for the
longer speakers (see diagram 3). Use
the remainder to cut a rectangle,
18 x 2 cm, and another 18 x 4 cm.
Use these for the radio and for the
switch panel.
5.  Cut five small squares, each
2 x 1.5 cm and use these for the
control buttons. Cut one last

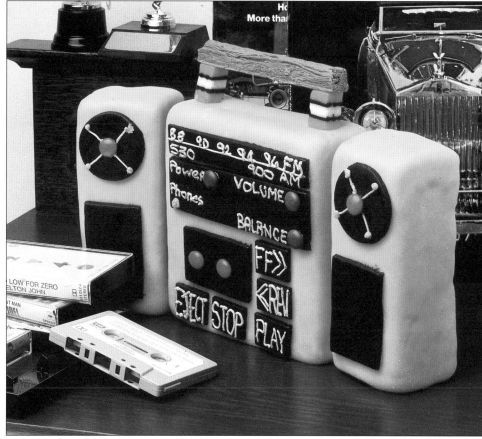

*The Ghetto Blaster*

rectangle 8 x 4 cm for the cassette
itself. Mix a little black food colouring
with water to form a paste. Paint all
these small pieces with this.
6.  Brush the positions for each of the
buttons with warm jam, and place the
buttons appropriately. Mix the icing
sugar and water together to form a

stiff paste of piping consistency. Pipe
in the numerals, lines and words as
shown. Place Smarties in position.
Stand the Ghetto Blaster on a cake
board. Put two licorice allsorts on top
of the main cake and balance the
chocolate bar between them securing
with icing if necessary.

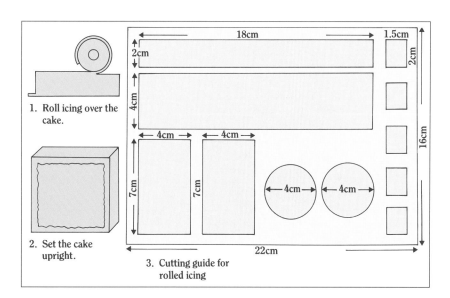

1.  Roll icing over the cake.

2.  Set the cake upright.

3.  Cutting guide for rolled icing

# FavouritePartyFare

Sometimes a theme is not the order of the day and a simple party at home is what the young host or the parents want.

A variety of party food will make the event a special occasion. Included in this selection of recipes are Fairy Bread and Sausage Rolls, both perennial party favourites. Sandwiches cut into alphabet shapes, with the yummiest of fillings, are always welcome. Frozen Strawberry Pops are easy to make and should have the most pernickety eater coming back for more.

## FRUITY MILK SHAKE

*Preparation time:* 5 minutes
*Cooking time:* nil
*Serves 6*
*Easy*

1 litre milk, chilled
1 cup fresh orange juice, chilled
4 passionfruit or granadillas
vanilla ice-cream

1.  Put milk, orange juice and passionfruit pulp into the container of a blender. Cover and blend for about 15 seconds.
2.  Pour into tumblers. Serve each with a scoop of ice-cream.

*Clockwise from top left: Fruity Milkshake, Sausage Rolls, Alphabet Sandwiches, Fairy Bread, Frozen Strawberry Pops, Cream Cheese Shapes and Traffic Lights (centre)*

*Frozen Strawberry Pops*

1. Spread bread thinly with butter. Sprinkle liberally with hundreds and thousands. Press down topping gently to make sprinkles adhere to bread.
2. To serve: remove crusts from bread and cut diagonally into quarters.

VARIATIONS
Instead of butter and hundreds and thousands use
*peanut butter and coloured sprinkles
*peanut-chocolate spread and toasted coconut
*honey and crushed chocolate-honeycomb bars

2. Cut each sandwich into the shape of a different letter of the alphabet, using a sharp pointed knife. Skewer each sandwich with a toothpick or small flag with the individual child's name written on it.
3. Cover with plastic wrap, damp greaseproof paper or a lightly damp tea towel to prevent sandwiches from drying out.

FILLINGS
*Tuna and Cress*
Drain 1 x 425 g can tuna; mix together with 2 tablespoons mayonnaise and a squeeze of lemon juice. Divide between 10 slices bread. Top with cress or fresh mung bean sprouts.

*Cheese, Date and Honey*
Combine together 500 g softened cream cheese, 2 tablespoons honey and 5 tablespoons chopped walnuts. Beat together until light and fluffy. Spread over 10 slices bread and top with 250 g chopped pitted dates.

*Peanut Butter and Jam*
Spread 10 slices bread thickly with peanut butter. Spread remaining 10 slices with a little jam. Join each slice of peanut buttered bread with a slice of bread and jam

## FROZEN STRAWBERRY POPS

*Preparation time:* 30 minutes plus freezing time
*Cooking time:* 3 minutes
*Makes about 20*
*Easy*

1 x 250 g punnet strawberries
125 g white chocolate
½ x 85 g packet strawberry jelly crystals
lollipop sticks

1. Rinse strawberries under cold water and pat dry with absorbent paper. Remove green stems. Insert lollipop stick in the core end of each strawberry. Place in the refrigerator to chill.
2. Melt white chocolate in a bowl over hot water. Remove from the heat and cool slightly. Stir thoroughly. Dip strawberries into chocolate and allow excess to drip back into bowl. Then dip into jelly crystals. Stand strawberry pops in freezer by inserting sticks into a piece of polystyrene.
3. Freeze until firm.

## FAIRY BREAD

*Preparation time:* 15 minutes
*Cooking time:* nil
*Serves 10*
*Easy*

10 slices bread
butter for spreading
1 cup hundreds and thousands

## ALPHABET SANDWICHES

*Preparation time:* 45 minutes
*Cooking time:* nil
*Serves 10*
*Easy*

1 loaf sliced bread
butter for spreading

1. Spread slices of bread thinly with butter. Spread 10 slices or half the loaf with the filling of your choice, and top with slices of buttered bread.

*Alphabet Sandwiches*

## SAUSAGE ROLLS

*Preparation time:* 35 minutes
*Cooking time:* 25 minutes
*Makes 48*
*Easy*

1 onion, finely chopped
1 teaspoon vegetable oil
500 g sausage mince
1 cup soft white breadcrumbs
2 tablespoons tomato sauce
1 egg, lightly beaten
3 sheets frozen, ready rolled puff
    pastry, thawed
egg or milk for glazing

*Sausage Rolls*

1.  Preheat oven to 220°C. Lightly grease an oven tray.
2.  Sauté onion in oil over low heat until onion is soft and transparent. In a bowl mix together onion, mince, breadcrumbs, tomato sauce and egg.
3.  Lay three sheets of pastry on a lightly floured board and cut in thirds horizontally. Divide the meat mixture into six equal portions and spoon across the long edge of the pastry. Roll up to form a long sausage shape. Brush lightly with a little beaten egg or milk to glaze. Cut into 4 cm lengths and place on prepared tray.

4.  Bake for 10 minutes, reduce heat to 180°C and bake a further 15 minutes until rolls are golden. Serve warm with tomato sauce.

HINTS
Freeze uncooked sausage rolls and bake as many as required directly from the freezer.

Bake sausage rolls ahead of time and reheat at 150°C for 5–10 minutes until heated through.

If taking these on a picnic, place the warm rolls in a covered polystyrene container, with a hot-water bottle filled with boiling water.

## CREAM CHEESE SHAPES

*Preparation time:* 30 minutes
*Cooking time:* 20 minutes
*Serves 10*
*Easy*

10 slices bread
250 g cream cheese, softened
2 tablespoons sour cream
1 tablespoon icing sugar
spread e.g. jam, honey, lemon butter
topping e.g. Smarties, marshmallows,
    raisins or sultanas or shredded
    coconut

1.  Preheat oven to 150°C. Cut out shapes of bread using a variety of biscuit cutters. Arrange bread shapes on a flat oven tray and bake for 15–20 minutes until bread is crispy but still pale. Remove from oven and cool.
2.  Beat together cream cheese, sour cream and icing sugar until light and fluffy.
3.  Fill a piping bag fitted with a small star pipe with cheese mixture. Pipe around the edge of the bread shapes. Spoon a little spread into the centre of the bread and decorate with your choice of topping.

HINT
For a delicious variation, use fruit loaf instead of plain bread. Spread dried fruit loaf shapes with cream cheese mixture and dust with cinnamon and sugar.

When drying the fruit loaf shapes in the oven keep a close eye on them — they could begin to brown due to the high sugar content.

*Cream Cheese Shapes*

## TRAFFIC LIGHTS

*Preparation time:* 30 minutes
*Cooking time:* nil
*Makes 24*
*Easy*

250 g processed or cheddar cheese
1 x 30 g packet of cheese flavoured
    biscuits
24 cherry tomatoes
6 gherkins, cut into quarters
small toothpicks or Twiglets

1.  Cut cheese into 24 even-sized cubes. Place biscuits in a bag and crush. Add cheese to bag and toss until coated with crumbs.
2.  Onto a toothpick or Twiglet thread one cherry tomato, one piece of cheese and one piece of gherkin. Repeat until all ingredients are used. Chill until ready to serve.

*Traffic Lights*

## BUTTER CAKE

*Preparation time:* 45 minutes
*Cooking time:* 45 minutes
*Easy*

125 g butter
¾ cup caster sugar
1 teaspoon vanilla essence
3 eggs
3 cups self-raising flour, sifted
½ cup milk

1.  Preheat oven to 180°C. Grease a 20 cm cake tin with melted butter, line with greaseproof paper and grease again.

Alternatively, prepare cake tins as directed in novelty cake recipe.
2.  Cream butter and sugar until pale, light and fluffy. Flavour with vanilla essence. Add eggs one at a time, beating well after each addition. Fold in flour and milk alternately beginning and finishing with flour.
3.  Spoon mixture into prepared tin and bake for 40–45 minutes or until cooked when tested. Remove from oven. Stand in tin for 5 minutes before turning out onto a wire rack to cool.

## OLD FASHIONED CHOCOLATE CAKE

*Preparation time:* 40 minutes
*Cooking time:* 45 minutes
*Easy*

60 g butter, softened
¾ cup caster sugar
1 egg
1 teaspoon vanilla essence
1½ cups self-raising flour
1 tablespoon cocoa
½ cup milk
¼ teaspoon bicarbonate of soda
¼ cup hot water

1.  Preheat oven to 180°C. Grease and line a square 20 cm cake tin with greaseproof paper and grease again. Alternatively, prepare cake tins as directed in novelty cake recipe.
2.  Cream butter and sugar together until blended (the mixture will not cream very well because of the high sugar to butter ratio).  Add egg and vanilla and beat well.
3.  Sift together flour and cocoa three times. Fold into butter mixture alternately with milk, beginning and ending with flour. Dissolve soda in hot water and fold into cake mixture.
4.  Pour into tin. Bake for 40–45 minutes or until cooked when tested. Stand for 5 minutes in tin before turning out to cool on a wire rack.

## BUTTER ICING

*Preparation time:* 10 minutes
*Cooking time:* nil
*Makes sufficient to cover and fill a 23 cm cake*
*Easy*

200 g butter
3 cups icing sugar
¼ teaspoon vanilla essence
1–2 tablespoons hot water

1.  Cream butter until light and fluffy. Beat in sifted icing sugar and vanilla essence until smooth. If necessary, add a little hot water to get a smooth spreading consistency.

VARIATIONS
*Chocolate:* sift icing sugar with 3 tablespoons cocoa.
*Orange:* mix through the finely grated zest of 1 orange and substitute fresh orange juice for the water.
*Peppermint:* add peppermint essence in place of vanilla.
*Coffee:* dissolve 3 teaspoons coffee powder in the hot water.

## BUTTERCREAM FROSTING

*Preparation time:* 20 minutes
*Cooking time:* nil
*Makes sufficient to ice a 20 cm cake*
*Easy*

This rich frosting is suitable to use as a filling as well as a cake covering. It is always best to use unsalted butter, which gives a sweeter, creamier frosting.

125 g softened butter
1 teaspoon vanilla essence
1½ cups icing sugar, sifted
2 tablespoons cream

1.  Beat butter until pale and creamy. Add vanilla and half the icing sugar and beat until combined. Gradually add milk and remaining sugar, beating until smooth.

## GLACÉ ICING

*Preparation time:* 10 minutes
*Cooking time:* 5 minutes
*Makes sufficient to cover 1 x 23 cm cake*
*Easy*

This is a very shiny icing that gives a smooth finish. The icing must be warmed first so that it becomes thin and runny. Pour over the cake immediately. To avoid cracking the smooth surface, try not to move the cake until the icing has set. This icing may also be used for piping but is then not warmed first.

2 cups icing sugar, sifted
2–3 tablespoons water
flavouring essence
food colouring

1.  Place sugar in a bowl. Beat in water and essence to form a smooth thick paste. Colour with a little food

colouring, adding gradually until the desired colour is reached. The icing is now ready for piping.

2. To use as an icing, place bowl over a pan of simmering water and heat until mixture is runny and shiny. Pour immediately over the surface of the cake to be iced. Guide icing with a hot wet spatula. Allow icing to set before moving the iced cake.

## TO COLOUR SUGAR

Place the required amount of crystal or caster sugar into a large strong bag or a large screwtop jar, add a few drops of food colouring and seal bag or replace lid of jar. Shake vigorously until colour is evenly dispersed and the desired colour is obtained. Add a little more food colouring if necessary.

## TO COLOUR COCONUT

Place the required amount of shredded or desiccated coconut into a large jar or strong bag. Add a few drops of food colouring. If the food colouring is a very intense in colour, dilute it with a little cold water. Place lid on jar or seal bag firmly, and shake vigorously until colour is evenly dispersed. If colour does not disperse evenly, wear a clean pair of disposable gloves or wear a clean plastic bag on each hand, and work the colour through with your hands.

## CUTTING SHAPES OF LICORICE AND ANGELICA

Lots of great shapes can be made from licorice and angelica. Cut these shapes using sharp scissors dipped in very hot water. Pinking shears will give a decorative edge. A sharp knife will work equally well but requires a little more care.

## HOW TO MAKE A PIPING BAG

1. Cut a 20 cm square of heavy greaseproof paper. Fold in half diagonally to form a triangle. Run a sharp knife along the folded edge to cut cleanly.
2. Take corner (1) and roll it so it lies inside the corner (2).
3. Bring unfolded corner (3) around the outside of the rolled cone so the edges line up together.
4. Gently pull corner (3) upwards to give bag a tight, firm tip.
5. Secure with tape and fold over top of bag.
6. Fill bag with icing or other filling and snip a small piece off the tip.

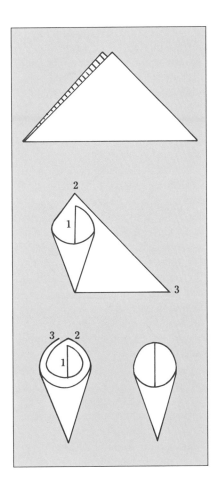

## CAKE BOARDS

It can be difficult to find a suitable board or plate for children's birthday cakes. However, there is all sorts of equipment that can do the job. Generally, a board has to be fairly large to accommodate the size of the cake together with surrounding decorations. The board is usually covered to enhance the appearance of the cake, protect the board, and prevent oil or fat oozing through from the frostings and cakes.

Suitable boards include:
*pieces of masonite — ideal for cake boards; a hardware or timber shop will usually cut them to the required size;
*an up-turned dinner tray providing a flat surface; this is often large enough for the cake;
*a flat oven slide or baking tray;
*a large chopping board;
*the outside of a large cardboard box which has been used for packaging large electrical appliances;
*large pieces of polystyrene used in packaging.

Suitable board coverings include:
*coloured shiny wrapping paper;
*foil, smooth or scrunched to give an uneven surface;
*silver or gold cake paper available from icing specialist shops and health food shops;
*coloured fabric. (Often, however, fat will ooze out of the cake and frosting and stain the cloth);
*a board spread with a thin layer of icing and sprinkled with coconut, hundreds and thousands, chocolate sprinkles, silver cachous, a mixture of sweets or coloured popcorn;
*a board sprayed with gloss paint. Ensure that the board is thoroughly dry before putting the cake on it.

# Sweets and Candy

SWEETS MAKE a delicious treat for children to take home after parties, and excellent prizes for party games. Commercially made sweets are a quick alternative for filling sweet bags, but home-made treats have an added charm and flavour. Some of these recipes can be made by the party host, others could be made with help from you.

Confectionery can be attractively presented in a variety of ways. Put some in a paper cup or a tiny basket, cover with cellophane and add a flourish of curly ribbon; or use paper serviettes or coloured paper, twisted into cones. Larger treats can be individually wrapped and tied with ribbon.

Children enjoy making their own sweet bags. Give them a good supply of paints, felt-tipped pens, coloured pencils and crayons, and an assortment of brown and white paper bags and let their imaginations run wild. Add a selection of scissors and glue (supervise younger children), tape, glitter, stars and stickers, used gift-wrap, old greeting cards, recycled boxes and containers.

Alternatively, make packaging from small lunch bags or cellophane packets. Make cardboard baskets decorated with hand-drawn patterns, or a collage of pictures cut from old magazines. Margarine tubs can be decorated with stickers and glitter. Try filling an ice-cream cone with sweets, then wrapping it in cellophane. If you have oddments of felt, fabric or tulle left over from sewing, use them to make pouches or small loot bags.

Filled sweet bags can be prepared well ahead of time. Toffee-based treats such as toffee apples, praline, sesame crunch and popcorn pearls should be stored in a dry place, particularly in humid weather. Alternatively, prepare them on the day of the party, or one day before.

Children enjoy helping in the preparation and cooking of sweets, but remember that hot sugar mixtures do reach very high temperatures, and can inflict serious burns if they are accidentally spilt or splashed. Young children, particularly, need help and a watchful eye if they volunteer as sweet-makers.

## SECRETS FOR SUCCESS
Confectionery is not difficult to make provided a few rules are applied:

* Use heavy-based pans when making toffee or syrups.

* Choose wooden spoons for stirring sugar syrups as they do not transfer heat, nor do they discolour the pan.

* Prior to cooking, have utensils and ingredients ready. You will need to work very quickly before the mixture begins to set, so time is a crucial factor.

* A candy thermometer, although not essential, does take the guesswork out of cooking sugar syrups. If using one, place it in a saucepan of water and bring to the boil. Meanwhile, bring the sugar syrup to the boil in another pan. After the syrup has boiled, transfer the candy thermometer to the syrup; clip it to the side of the pan. Watch the temperature carefully, particularly as the mixture approaches the required heat.

*When making toffee-based sweets or boiling a sugar syrup it is essential to dissolve the sugar prior to the mixture boiling. Do this by bringing the syrup slowly to the boil, and stirring until the sugar is dissolved. Wash undissolved sugar crystals down the side of the pan with a pastry brush dipped in water.

*Unless the recipe advises otherwise, avoid stirring a sugar syrup after it has come to the boil.

*In humid weather, remember that sugar mixtures take longer to cook. After cooking, store in a dry place to prevent the confectionery from becoming syrupy.

## DECORATIONS
When confectionery has been made, decorate it with hundreds and thousands, coconut, silver cachous, cherries, chopped nuts, licorice, melted or grated chocolate, sesame seeds, dried fruits or coloured sugar.

*Clockwise from upper left: Frozen Moments, Toffee Apples, Speckled Bubble Bars, Fast Chocolate Fudge, Sesame Crunch, Toffees, Popcorn Pearls and Coconut Roughs. Centre: Coconut Ice, New Orleans Pralines.*

*Frozen Moments*

## FROZEN MOMENTS

*Preparation time*: 35 minutes
*Cooking time*: 15 minutes
*Makes 20*
*Easy*

2 cups white sugar
2 tablespoons gelatine
2 cups cold water
vanilla essence
20 coloured ice cream cones
375 g mixed sweets

1.  Place sugar, gelatine and water in a pan. Bring slowly to the boil stirring until sugar dissolves. Boil for 10 minutes, remove from heat and cool.
2.  Stir in essence and beat with an electric mixer until mixture is thick and fluffy. Drop a few sweets into the base of each cone and fill with marshmallow mixture. Decorate with sweets and shredded coconut. When marshmallow cools it will set firm.

## SESAME CRUNCH

*Preparation time*: 20 minutes
*Cooking time*: 20 minutes
*Makes 24*
*Easy*

2 cups sesame seeds
½ cup honey
½ cup sugar
½ teaspoon ground ginger
½ teaspoon cinnamon

1.  Line a 28 x 18 cm shallow tin with greaseproof paper and brush lightly with oil. Place sesame seeds in a frypan and stir over low heat until lightly toasted. Cool.
2.  Combine remaining ingredients in another pan. Cook over low heat, stirring until sugar dissolves and mixture boils. Boil for 2 minutes without stirring. Fold in sesame seeds and pour at once into prepared tin, spreading evenly. Cool 15–20 minutes.
3.  Remove crunch from tin with paper attached. With a sharp knife, cut into small fingers or squares. Cool completely, then peel off paper. Wrap pieces individually.

## TOFFEE

*Preparation time*: 20 minutes
*Cooking time*: 15 minutes
*Makes 24*
*Easy*

1 cup water
4 cups sugar
1 tablespoon vinegar
hundreds and thousands or coconut
    for decoration

1.  Heat water, sugar and vinegar in a pan, stirring until sugar dissolves. Brush any sugar crystals down sides of pan with a wet pastry brush.
2.  Bring to the boil. Cook, without stirring, until mixture turns golden or reaches 132°C.
3.  Pour into paper cake cases and allow to set. Decorate as desired.

*Toffee*

## SPECKLED BUBBLE BARS

*Preparation time*: 20 minutes
*Cooking time*: 5 minutes
*Makes 24*
*Easy*

1½ cups marshmallows
60 g butter
½ teaspoon peppermint essence
2½ cups Rice Crispies
½ cup hundreds and thousands

1.  Line an 18 x 28 cm shallow tin with foil or baking paper and grease lightly. Place marshmallows and butter in a small pan. Stir over low heat until melted. Remove from heat.
2.  Stir in essence. Place Rice Crispies and hundreds and thousands in a large bowl. Pour in marshmallow mixture and mix well.
3.  Pour into prepared tin and spread out evenly with a spatula. Cool and cut into squares.

## COCONUT ROUGHS

*Preparation time*: 10 minutes
*Cooking time*: 1 minute
*Makes 36*
*Easy*

125 g copha
¾ cup icing sugar, sifted
½ cup cocoa
⅓ cup dried milk powder
1 cup desiccated coconut

1.  Lightly brush a flat oven tray with oil. Melt copha over low heat. Mix together all remaining ingredients and pour in melted copha. Mix until well combined.
2.  Place teaspoonfuls of mixture on prepared tray. Refrigerate until set.

## NEW ORLEANS PRALINES

*Preparation time*: 25 minutes
*Cooking time*: 20 minutes
*Makes 24*
*Medium*

2 cups sugar
⅔ cup milk
⅓ cup dark corn syrup
½ teaspoon vanilla essence
1 cup pecan pieces

*Speckled Bubble Bars*

1. Combine sugar, milk and syrup in a heavy-based pan. Stir over low heat until sugar dissolves and mixture comes to the boil. Continue boiling until a teaspoonful of syrup dropped into cold water can be shaped into a soft ball or until mixture reaches 112°–118°C.
2. Remove from heat and cool to lukewarm. Add vanilla and beat with wooden spoon until mixture begins to thicken. Stir in pecans.
3. Spoon small portions onto greaseproof paper, flattening each slightly. Stand until set.

## COCONUT ICE

*Preparation time:* 20 minutes
*Cooking time:* nil
*Makes 20 pieces*
*Easy*

1 x 410 g can condensed milk
1 tablespoon strawberry essence
3⅓ cups icing sugar, sifted
4 cups desiccated coconut
pink food colouring

1. Combine condensed milk, essence, icing sugar and coconut in a bowl and mix well.
2. Divide mixture into halves. Colour one half pale pink and press firmly into a lightly oiled bar tin. Top with remaining mixture and chill until firm. Cut into squares for serving.

## TOFFEE APPLES

*Preparation time:* 50 minutes
*Cooking time:* 20 minutes
*Makes 20*
*Medium*

20 red apples
1 cup water
4 cups sugar
1 tablespoon vinegar
4 teaspoons powdered red food colouring or 2 tablespoons cochineal

1. Wash, dry and polish apples. Place a 15 cm skewer into the centre of each apple.
2. Combine remaining ingredients in a pan. Bring slowly to the boil, stirring until sugar dissolves. Boil, without stirring, until mixture becomes brittle when a little of it is dropped into iced water.
3. Dip apples into toffee and swirl around until coated. Drain. Cool on a sheet of greased foil until toffee sets.

## POPCORN PEARLS

*Preparation time:* 1½ hours
*Cooking time:* 30 minutes
*Makes 12 x 50 cm lengths*
*Medium*

⅓ cup vegetable oil
1 cup uncooked popcorn
1 cup white sugar
1 tablespoon honey
1 tablespoon golden syrup
½ cup water
60 g butter

1. Heat oil in a large pan, add popcorn and cover pan with a lid. Place over moderate heat and cook, shaking pan occasionally. When popping stops, all the popcorn is cooked. Transfer to a large bowl, removing unpopped corn.
2. Combine remaining ingredients in a heavy-based pan and bring slowly to the boil, stirring until the sugar dissolves. Wash undissolved crystals down sides of pan with a wet pastry brush. Ensure all the sugar dissolves before mixture boils. Boil until mixture reaches 150°C. Test by dropping a small amount of mixture in iced water — it should turn hard and brittle.

3. Pour over popcorn and mix until well coated. Continue stirring until mixture sets and cools slightly. Place on large tray to cool.
4. Cut 12 x 50 cm lengths of heavy cotton. Using a thick needle, thread individual pieces of popcorn on cotton to make strings of popcorn, continuing until thread is completely covered. Tie ends together.

HINT
You can omit steps 2 and 3 and simply sprinkle the popcorn with a little icing sugar or garlic powder and then thread on cotton if you prefer.

## FAST CHOCOLATE FUDGE

*Preparation time:* 15 minutes plus chilling time
*Cooking time:* 5 minutes
*Makes about 49*
*Easy*

125 g dark compound cooking chocolate, chopped
125 g copha, chopped
2 tablespoons icing sugar
1 tablespoon cocoa
½ x 420 g can sweetened condensed milk
½ teaspoon vanilla essence

1. Line the base of an 18 cm square cake tin with greaseproof paper or foil. Oil lightly.
2. Melt together chocolate and copha over a low heat, stirring until smooth.
3. Quickly stir in remaining ingredients until blended (mixture will begin to firm immediately).
4. Pour at once into prepared tin; smooth the surface. Chill until firm. Cut into squares to serve.

*Fast Chocolate Fudge*

# Party Games

CHILDREN LOVE party games. Adults enjoy them too. For a successful party, have a varied programme of games prepared in advance. Keep things moving by having all necessary equipment to play the games — thimbles, counters or blindfolds — ready before guests arrive. When things get boisterous, introduce a few quiet games.

Remember to have lots of small prizes ready. One way of presenting these is to fill a deep bowl with assorted small items — fancy pencils and rubbers, small chocolate bars, whistles, candy canes — and let children choose their prizes with their eyes closed, on a lucky dip basis.

## MUSICAL GAMES

Traditional musical games are familiar and popular, especially with pre-school children, and help break down the shyness barrier. Often, the same game is played repeatedly without any signs of boredom. Let them continue until they tire of it, then move on to the next game.

### Ring-a-Ring-of-Roses

Players form a circle and join hands, then skip around singing the verse. At the words 'fall down' they all collapse on the floor. For older children, ring the changes by making the last player to fall be 'out'.

*Ring-a-ring-of-roses*
*A pocketful of posies*
*A tishoo! A tishoo!*
*We all fall down.*

### Oranges and Lemons

One player elects to be an orange, the other a lemon. They form an arch by holding hands above head level. While all sing the rhyme, the other players file behind each other, continually passing under the arch. With the words 'chop off your head', the two children forming the arch move their arms down to capture the child who is walking through the arch at the time. That one selects a side — oranges or lemons — and stands behind the appropriate part of the arch. The pattern continues until all are captured. Oranges then have a tug-of-war with the lemons. The rhyme is:

*'Oranges and lemons,'*
*Say the bells of St. Clements.*
*'You owe me five farthings,'*
*Say the bells of St. Martins.*
*'When will you pay me?'*
*Say the bells of Old Bailey.*
*'When I grow rich,'*
*Say the bells of Shoreditch.*
*'When will that be?'*
*Ask the bells of Stephney.*
*'I'm sure I don't know,'*
*Says the great bell of Bow.*

*Here comes a candle to light you*
*    to bed,*
*Here comes a chopper to chop off*
*    your head.*

### The Farmer in the Dell

There are several variations of this game, sometimes known as *The Farmer in his Den*. The farmer is chosen. The other children form a

circle and walk around the farmer singing:

*The farmer's in the dell,*
*The farmer's in the dell,*
*Hey ho, the dairy-o,*
*The farmer's in the dell.*

*The farmer wants a wife,*
*The farmer wants a wife,*
*Hey ho, the dairy-o,*
*The farmer wants a wife.*

The farmer in the centre then chooses a partner to stand inside the circle with him.

The verse is repeated with the following substitutions:

*The wife wants a child;*
*The child wants a nurse;*
*The nurse wants a dog.*

Each time, the last nominated child chooses another one to step into the circle. Finally everyone sings

*We all pat the dog,*
*We all pat the dog,*
*Hey ho, the dairy-o,*
*We all pat the dog.*

Everyone then proceeds to pat the dog on the back. The game starts all over again, usually with the dog becoming the farmer.

### Here We Go Round the Mulberry Bush

This is a game in which the children mime the different actions as they sing about them. In a circle, they dance and sing:

*Here we go round the mulberry bush,*
*The mulberry bush, the mulberry*
*  bush,*
*Here we go round the mulberry bush,*
*On a cold and frosty morning.*

Then they stop, and as they sing they mime:

*This is the way we wash our clothes*
*Wash our clothes, wash our clothes,*
*This is the way we wash our clothes*
*On a cold and frosty morning.*

Each child or an adult then sings the first line of a new verse and as everyone sings the rest, the actions are mimed. Some suggestions are:

*This is the way we polish our shoes.*
*This is the way we wash our hands.*
*This is the way we clean our teeth.*
*This is the way we iron our clothes.*
*This is the way we drink our tea.*
*This is the way we pat our cat.*
*This is the way we walk to school.*

Keep the actions familiar and children will probably want to play the game for some time. When they run out of ideas, stop the game and start another.

### Three Blind Mice

Children join hands to form a circle round a child in the centre, who is chosen to be the farmer's wife. The children skip or dance round singing:

*Three blind mice,*
*Three blind mice,*
*See how they run,*
*See how they run,*
*They all run after the farmer's wife*
*Who cuts off their tails with a carving*
*  knife.*
*Did you ever see such a thing in your*
*  life*
*As three blind mice?*

At the end of the last line, the farmer's wife tries to catch someone. The mouse then joins the farmer's wife in the centre and the game begins again until all the children have been caught. If the game starts over again, the first child caught becomes the farmer's wife.

### When-the-Music-Stops Games

Ideally the person stopping and starting the music should be hidden from the players. However, a little judicious cheating ensures that every young child receives a prize.

### Pass the Parcel

The players sit round in a circle. A prize, wrapped in several layers of paper, is passed round from player to player as music plays. When the music stops, the child holding the parcel unwraps one layer. Then the music starts again and the passing continues. Eventually the music stops for the last layer of wrapping, leaving the winner holding the prize. For very young children, place a sweet at every layer to hold their interest.

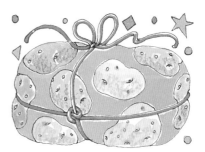

### Hot Potato

Players sit in a circle. A smooth object such as a plastic ball is quickly passed round as the music plays. When the music stops the player holding the object is eliminated from the circle. Another variation of this is *Musical Torch*; lights are turned out, and as the music plays a torch is passed at just under chin level so that the face of each child is lit up. Whoever is left holding the torch when the music stops has to drop out. A stout plastic torch is best, as it may be dropped.

### Musical Bumps

Players caper about as music plays. When it stops, all players must immediately sit down. Last one to sit is out. The game goes on until only the winner is left.

### Musical Statues

This game is similar to *Musical Bumps*. When the music stops, the children have to 'freeze' in position and remain as still as statues. Anyone who twitches is out.

### Musical Chairs

Two rows of chairs are placed back to back. The players march around the groups of chairs in the same direction in time to the music. When the music stops everyone must sit down, but there is one chair less. The person without a chair drops out. A chair is removed and the game starts again. The game continues until only two players are left competing for one chair.

Another variation of this is *Musical Cushions*. (Cushions are easier to move than chairs, too.)

### Musical Hats

A funny game which is rather like *Musical Chairs*, but is played with a hat for each player, except one. Everyone stands or sits in a circle, facing in the same direction. When the music starts, each player takes the hat from the head of the person in front and puts it on. When the music stops the person without a hat is eliminated. Remove one hat and continue the game until only one person is left with a hat.

### Jump the Broom

Put a broom on the ground. Play music as the children skip round in a circle, jumping over the broom each time they come to it. When the music stops, the child jumping over the broom, or the last child to jump the broom is out. Continue until there is one child left.

### Musical Sets

All players skip round the room as the music plays. When the music stops a number is called and they scramble to form sets of that number. Call out a number that must leave one child out; for example, call 'four' for 17 children and four sets will form with one child remaining. That player drops out. With the number fifteen you could call out seven and one more player would be eliminated.

## OTHER FAVOURITES

### String Hunt

This is a good game to warm up a young party as it will keep the early arrivals occupied while waiting for the other guests to arrive. Allow a ball of string for each guest; tie one end of it to a small present and place the present where it can be seen. Unwind the ball of string, making a trail across chairs, under tables, around door knobs, under rugs and so on, making it tricky and moderately tangled, depending on the age group. As the guests arrive, each is given her ball of string and she starts to wind up the string. The string trail is followed until the present at the end is reached. It is a good idea to put breakables out of the way while the game is in progress.

### Follow the Leader

A simple non-competitive game that delights young children and is a good one to get a young party moving. With some music playing, an adult leads the line of children around the house or garden either skipping, hopping or jogging and performing odd actions which the children copy. Crawl under tables, jump over benches and skip in and out of trees. The more varied, the better.

### Froggy, Froggy, May We Cross Your Shining River?

One child is elected to be Froggy, and stands with back turned to the rest of the group. Two parallel lines are marked with a good space — about 4–5 metres — between them. Froggy stands behind the line on one side, and the rest of the group stands behind the line on the other side.

Together, the group chants, 'Froggy, Froggy, may we cross your shining river?'

Froggy responds, 'Not unless you wear the colour — BLUE!' or, 'Not unless you wear — GREEN SOCKS!' or whatever Froggy chooses. At the chosen word — 'BLUE!' or 'GREEN SOCKS!' — Froggy turns quickly to face the rest of the group, and the child or children wearing the nominated colour or clothing have to race across the river without being caught by Froggy. The child who is caught becomes the next Froggy, and the last frog returns to the group.

### Pin the Tail on the Donkey

Draw an outline of a donkey without a tail on a large sheet of cardboard. Mark a spot where the tail should be. Place in a position where the children can reach. Each child in turn is given the donkey's tail with a drawing pin in one end. The child is blindfolded, spun round, steps forward and tries to pin the tail in the appropriate spot. The position is marked with the child's initial and the next child has a turn. The one who puts the tail on, or nearest to, the correct spot, wins.

### What's the Time, Mr Wolf?

A chasing game that is best played outdoors. One player or an adult is chosen to be Mr Wolf. A den or safe place is chosen at the start. Mr Wolf prowls around followed by the rest of the children who keep calling, 'What's the time, Mr Wolf?' Mr Wolf must answer with a time of the day such as one o'clock, six o'clock, four o'clock and so on. When Mr Wolf, at his discretion, growls 'Dinner time' the children must dash for the den. If the wolf catches anyone before they reach the safety area, the victim becomes the next Mr Wolf. Alternatively, this game can be played by elimination. Each child caught sits down. The last player to be caught becomes the wolf for the next round.

### Pass the Oranges

Arrange for two teams to stand in line with each person behind the other.

Each team is given an orange. The orange is to be passed down the line from one player to another without using hands. To do so, it is held by each player under the chin and transferred to the chin of the next player.

If at any point the orange is dropped, it must be returned to the front of the line and passing starts all over again.

The first team to complete passing the orange to all members, wins.

## Sardines

An extremely popular hide and seek game that can be played indoors or outside. All players except one count to 100 together. The odd one out goes into hiding. All then hunt for the hidden player. When discovered, the finder does not shout out but joins the person in hiding. In the end, all seekers have become hiders, squashed into one hiding place with much hilarity. The first seeker to find the hiding place becomes the first hider in the next game.

## Blowing Bubbles

Very young children are fascinated with bubbles. A supply of plastic bubble pipes and liquid can keep them amused for some time. Bubbles are best blown outdoors. It can be made competitive by seeing who can blow the biggest bubble, or whose bubble lasts the longest.

## Guessing Competition

Place a number of small colourful sweets such as jelly beans in a glass jar. Ask each guest to guess how many sweets there are in the jar. The child with the nearest guess wins the jar.

## On the Bank, In the River

A lively game for young children. Line them up behind a marked line. The side they are standing on is the bank, the other side is the river. Call out 'in the river' or 'on the bank', mixing up the commands. Children have to jump to the correct side. Those who do not are out.

## Scavenger Chase

Depending on the age of the children, the game list can be made simple for very young children who have just begun to read, or quite complicated for older children. The idea of the game is to give each player (or pair of players) a list of objects to collect within a determined length of time. A good idea is to write the list on a paper bag, which can be used for collecting. The first to collect all the items on their list wins. A simple list might include a piece of string, a

flower, a gum leaf, a round stone, a feather and so on.

A variation of this game is an Alphabet Hunt; each player is given or chooses a letter of the alphabet, and has to collect things beginning with that letter.

## Trains and Stations

One person is chosen to sit in the middle of a circle of players who are holding hands with their arms crossed. Another person in the circle is chosen as the leader who sets the train off. Two people in the circle are 'stations'. The train is sent around the circle by a squeeze of the hand and every time it passes a station the person says, 'toot toot'. The train can be sent in the same direction or sent back by squeezing the hand on the side where the train just came from. The aim of the person in the middle is to guess which person has the train at any particular moment. If their guess is correct, then the person caught with the train has to go into the middle. Stations should be changed at changeover of players.

## Fishing Competition

You will need an assortment of coloured fish cut out from light cardboard. The host will enjoy making these before the party. Attach

a safety pin to the nose of each fish. Write a number on the back of each fish to represent its weight and arrange them all in a large shallow dish which represents the lake. Turn them over so that the numbers cannot be seen. Give each player a fishing rod, made by tying a small magnet on to the end of a pencil with a piece of cotton or light string. On the starting signal, all the players take their rods and try to catch as many fish as they can. When they are all caught, everyone adds up the total weight of the fish they have caught. The player with the highest score wins.

## Wobbling Bunnies

A fun game for very young children. Players make their hands into ears at the sides of their heads and bunny-hop about, pretending to be rabbits. At the call of 'Danger', they freeze, and must keep absolutely still for the count of five. Any player who twitches a whisker during the count, is out.

## QUIET GAMES

When things get rowdy, your nerves are fraying and a change of pace is needed, these quieter games can be introduced to vary the activities and keep the children's interest. They can also be played for a short period after the meal on wet days. Some of these games will also come in handy during school holidays, when travelling or on weekends.

## I Spy

A child starts the game by silently choosing an object that can be seen in the room, then saying the first letter of its name. For example, if it's the clock, the child will say, 'I spy with my little eye something beginning with C'. The first player to guess the correct answer chooses the next object and starts the next round.

Alternatively, the game can be played with pencil and paper. All players are asked to write down as many things as can be seen all beginning with a certain letter. This can be played several times, finding a winner each time.

### O'Grady Says

Also known as *Simon Says*. All players face O'Grady (or Simon) who performs various actions and gives an instruction that should begin with 'O'Grady says'. Some instructions deliberately omit the phrase, for example, 'O'Grady says touch your toes' or 'Hold your nose'. The children must only copy instructions prefaced by 'O'Grady says'. Players who perform an action that does not begin with 'O'Grady says' are out. The last child remaining is the winner.

### Memory Test

Make a selection of about twenty common objects such as a spoon, key, button, book, sweet, pen, paperclip, safety pin etc. Place them on a tray and cover them with a cloth. Give each player a pencil and paper. The players gather round and the cloth is removed for two minutes. Then the tray is taken away. The players have to write down as many objects as they can remember. The player who makes the longest correct list within a set time limit is the winner.

### Hangman

Pin a big piece of paper on a board. Think of a word of more than seven letters that the children will recognise, such as *kangaroo* or *elephant*. Draw dashes at the top of the paper to represent the number of letters making up the word. As each player calls out a letter, and provided it is correct, write it in the appropriate place. If it is not correct, start drawing a hangman, one line for each wrong call. If the correct word is completed before the hangman is finished, the group wins and you lose.

### Paddy's Black Pig

This is great fun for a small group of children, or for playing one-to-one with a child.

The child, or group, are asked questions, to which they may only give one answer: 'Paddy's Black Pig.' Any child who smiles or giggles is out. Carefully framed questions form traps for the unwary;
'Who did you see when you looked in the mirror this morning?'
'Paddy's Black Pig'.
'Who's your best friend?'
'Paddy's Black Pig'.

Another version of this game is *Sausage*: instead of Paddy's Black Pig, the only answer that may be given is 'Sausage'.

### Hat Making

A quiet game for a small number of children, this works very well when played in pairs. Give each pair one newspaper, three sheets of coloured paper, twelve pins, a roll of sticky tape and a pair of scissors. The pairs are asked to produce a fancy hat in fifteen minutes, using only the given material. The winning hat is the one voted best by all the players.

### Feeling and Remembering

Fill a leg of a long thick sock with an assortment of about fifteen familiar objects such as a marble, cotton wool, matchbox, spoon, thimble, a walnut, a pencil and so on. In turn, the children are each given about a minute in which to feel the objects. Players then begin to write down as many objects as they could identify. The winner is the one who correctly identifies the most objects.

### What's Wrong?

This is best played with a small number of children in a fairly uncluttered room. Tell all the players to take careful notice of all the details in the room. Explain to them that you will make some alteration to the

room. Then send all the players outside and make your change, such as changing the chairs around, reversing the position of the vases, putting on a lamp light and so on. Call in the players and ask them to tell you what is wrong. The winner is the one with the first correct answer.

### Making Words

The players are given a reasonably long (but comprehensible) word, which they write at the top of their sheets of paper. They are then given a set time of about ten minutes in which to make up as many words as they can from the letters of the given word. Score by giving a point for each word. No word made must contain less than three letters. Determine before the game if scoring will be allowed for plural words which are formed by the addition of the letter 's'. Some useful words for this type of game are:
*alternative, Australian, chrysanthemum, curiosity, combination, consequence, dictionary, dishwasher, enormous, fantastic, grammatical, monumental, maximum, necessarily, observatory, procrastinate, rigmarole* and *theatrical.*

### Mystery Matchboxes

Fill each of eight matchboxes with the following or other materials of your choice:

1. nails
2. rice
3. matches
4. pins
5. peanuts
6. lentils
7. gravel
8. sugar crystals

Write the number on each box. Tell the players what the contents of the boxes are, but not which box contains which objects. Let the children make a note of the objects. They then shake the boxes and try to match the correct box number with the contents.

## GAMES WITH BALLOONS

### Balloon Fight

Every child is given a balloon. They have to throw their balloon into the air and keep it up there, while at the same time trying to knock other players' balloons to the ground. The winner is the last player with a balloon in the air.

### Whizzing Balloons

Each player stands behind a line and blows up a balloon of a different colour, or one marked with a player's name. The balloon is held at the neck to keep it inflated until the word 'Go' is called out. The balloons are then released to whiz forward. The balloon which travels the furthest wins.

### Blow the Balloon Race

Divide the children into two teams, each team with a round balloon and each child with a straw. Each team has a starting line. On their hands and knees, and blowing through the straw, each child chases the balloon along the ground from the starting line to a turning point and back again. The first team to finish wins.

### Broomstick Relay

Mark two parallel lines approximately three metres apart, and call one the starting line. Divide the children into pairs, then line them up opposite each other behind the line. Each child at the head of a starting line has a broom and a balloon. Each must sweep the balloon towards their opposite number, who must then sweep it back again. Bursting balloons disqualify sweepers, and the first pair to successfully complete the relay are the winners.

### Hop and Pop

Tie a balloon to one ankle of each player. Children have to burst each other's balloons while keeping their own intact. A player is disqualified once his or her balloon is burst.

### Knee Balloon Race

Players each have a book and a balloon. With the book balanced on their heads and the balloon held between their knees, they must race from starting point to finishing line. If balloon or book are dropped, they must start again. If a balloon bursts, the player is disqualified or must start again. For a large party the players can be divided into teams and a normal relay procedure used.

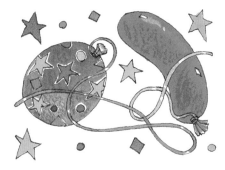

### Bat the Balloon

Divide the children into two teams and seat them, crossed legged on the floor and facing each other. The players must remain seated. The balloon is tossed between them and each team tries to tap the balloon over the heads of the opposite team, onto the ground behind their backs.

### Balloon Dress-ups

Everyone, including the onlookers, enjoys this funny game. Each child is provided with an uninflated balloon, a chair and a basket containing an old hat, gloves, socks, scarf, coat and an old nightie. There must be similar items of clothing in each basket. The baskets are placed opposite the players some distance away. The players are lined up at their chairs with the balloon. On the starting signal they must blow up the balloon and secure the end. Then, taking the balloon with them, they run to their basket and put on all the clothes. When completely dressed, they must run back to their chair and sit on their balloon until it bursts. The first player to burst the balloon is the winner. A tip for the children: the more inflated the balloon, the easier it is to burst.

## BLINDFOLD GAMES

After the age of four, most children enjoy blindfold games. Younger children can become quite frightened by them.

### Blind Man's Bluff

One player is blindfolded, spun around three times and left to catch one of the other players. The child must then guess, by feeling, who she has caught. If she guesses correctly, the caught child takes over as the Blind Man.

### Taste and Guess

Players are asked to go out of the room while six or more dishes of different things are laid out. They are then led in blindfolded, and asked to taste the different things. They have to guess what they think they've eaten. Only a small amount should be given to each player. Suitable substances are grated cheese, mint leaf, cold pasta, tiny pieces of orange, desiccated coconut, sliced tomato, a cocktail onion and so on. Each player who has finished can stay in the room and quietly watch the others. The person who correctly identifies the most dishes is the winner.

### Blindfold Drawing

Give each blindfolded player a piece of paper and a pencil, and a subject to draw, such as a house or a vase. When the players think they have completed their drawing, ask for some additions to be made, for example, 'Put a letterbox on the house' or 'Draw in the garden'. The winning picture is the one voted the most amusing or the best by the other players.

### Find the Bell-Ringer

One child is given a bell, and all the others are blindfolded. The sighted child then mingles among the blindfolded children, occasionally ringing the bell. Players do their best to catch the bell-ringer. The one who succeeds is the next bell-ringer, while the last bell-ringer joins the group of blindfolded children.

## GAMES FOR THE UNDER TWELVES

The following party games are enjoyed by the pre-teens and can be organised by the children themselves.

## Wrap the Mummy

Divide the players into two teams and choose a child of equal size for each team. This child is to be the Mummy. Get the players to stand in a row, behind a line about two metres from their mummy. The object of the game is for each team to completely wrap their mummy in toilet paper, until no clothes or skin show. The mummy must stand perfectly still, with arms close to the body and legs straight and closed.

On a starting signal, the first player of each team has two minutes to start wrapping the mummy. When the time is up, the roll of toilet paper is handed to the next player and the first wrapper must go to the end of the line. No helping is allowed. The team who first completes the wrapping of their mummy is the winner.

## Doughnut-Eating Race

Hang short lengths of string from the clothes line, one for each player. On each string tie a doughnut. The height of each doughnut must be adjusted so that the player has to stand on tiptoe to reach it with his mouth only. Hands must not be used. The first one to finish eating the whole doughnut wins.

## Chopsticks and Marbles

A game best played by small numbers of children. Place about thirty marbles in a large bowl with water in it. Each child is given a turn of two minutes' duration. Using the chopsticks, and only one hand, they have to pick out the marbles and transfer them to a smaller bowl. Write down the total number of marbles moved after each child's turn, before returning the marbles to the large bowl. The player who moves the most marbles is the winner.

Wooden chopsticks are the easiest to use.

## Consequence Drawing

Give each child a pencil and a long sheet of paper that has been folded into three sections. Ask them all to draw the head of a person on the top third. The paper is folded once, then passed to the next player, who draws a body on the middle third. This is then folded over, passed on, and they all draw the legs and feet. The paper is passed on for a final time and then opened out, with hilarious results.

## Apple Bobbing

Fill a large basin with water and float apples in it. Players kneel down and attempt to catch an apple using only their mouth. Each player who successfully removes an apple from the water may eat the apple. The winner is the player who first catches the apple. (This game must be supervised in case of accidental water inhalation.)

## Postman's Holiday

You will need ten boxes, each with a posting slot and labelled with a different town or street name. The boxes are hidden around the house or garden. Each player gets ten envelopes with the same ten place names. Starting from a common central point, players pick up one envelope at a time, write their initials on the back, then run off to post it in the right box. They then run back for another envelope. They must post their ten envelopes as fast as possible. When they have all done so, open the boxes and check the envelopes inside. The one with the most posted correctly, wins.

## The Chocolate Game

A hat, scarf and gloves, a knife, fork and plate, a bar of chocolate and a dice are needed for this game.

All players sit in a circle on the floor. In the centre of the circle is the hat, scarf and gloves with the bar of chocolate, and the knife and fork on the plate. In turn, each player throws a dice and when they throw a six, they rush to put on the hat, scarf and gloves. Then they try to both unwrap and eat the chocolate using only the knife and fork (no hands allowed). In the meantime, the other players are still taking turns to throw the dice. As soon as another player throws a six, they rush to remove the hat, scarf and gloves from the first player, put them on and continue to try to eat the chocolate. The first player rejoins the others. The game continues until all the chocolate has been eaten.

## The Ring Game

Arrange the players in a circle with one player in the middle. Players hold a circle of string, onto which is threaded a ring. At a signal to start, the centre player closes his eyes tightly and counts silently up to twenty. While this is being done, the players in the circle are sliding the ring from hand to hand round the string, all the time trying to conceal it under their hands. When the centre player has reached twenty, he opens his eyes and tries to spot which player is holding the ring. If guessed correctly, the player holding the ring changes places. If not, the player stays in the centre.

## Guess in the Dark

Another 'in the dark' game which is enjoyed by children aged about nine or ten.

All the players sit round a table and are provided with a pencil and paper. The lights are switched off, and an object is passed round the table from player to player. The lights are then switched on and the players write down what they think the object was. Provide about twelve very different and unusual objects, such as a hair conditioner sachet, an apricot, a plastic house fly, a bulb of garlic, a piece of pumice stone, a piece of sandpaper, a wrinkled passionfruit, or a large sinker. The person who correctly lists the most objects is the winner.

### Murder in the Dark

You will need pieces of paper, one for each player. Mark one with a 'D', another with an 'M', and leave the others blank. Fold the pieces of paper and put them in a hat. Each player draws one and looks at it without showing or telling anyone else what is on their piece of paper. Only the detective, who drew the D, takes position at the light switch. All lights are turned out. The room or house must be very dark. Other players move about the room. The murderer, who drew the M, approaches a player, grasps their arm and whispers 'You're dead'. The victim obligingly screams and falls down. All players must freeze, except the murderer, who tries to move away from the 'corpse'. At the count of five, the detective restores the light and tries to discover the murderer's identity. The detective can ask anyone as many questions as she likes. No players except the murderer may lie about their actions. Only the murderer can lie, but he must confess if the detective correctly solves the crime and asks, 'Are you the murderer?'

### Magpies

This is a miniature scavenger hunt that can be played throughout the duration of the party, whenever a player spots something to add to their collection.

At the very start of the party, each child is given a matchbox with their name on it. The object of the game is for each player to collect as many tiny things as they can fit into their matchbox. Grains of sand or sugar are not counted. At the end of the party the matchboxes are collected and the contents counted. The player who has collected the highest number of objects is the winner.

### The Flour Game

Tightly pack a kitchen bowl with flour and turn it out onto a plate so that there is a flour mountain. Stand the plate on some newspaper and put a blunt knife beside it. On top of the mountain place a sweet. Players take turns to cut away tiny slices of the mountain without making it collapse. When the mountain collapses and the sweet falls, the player responsible has to put his hands behind his back, bend over the place and eat the sweet from the flour.

### Hedgehogs

This is a funny game for all ages, and is especially useful at small parties.

Give each player a fairly large potato, a saucer of pins and a pair of gloves. Each player, wearing the gloves, is then required to pick up the pins one at a time and stick them into the potato. The one who has given the hedgehog the most spines in three minutes wins the competition.

### Charades

Charades is a popular miming game enjoyed by children of all ages. The idea is for one player to act out a word or a title, in mime, while onlookers try to guess the word. Having decided upon a word, the player acts or mimes a little sketch to illustrate each syllable of the word. For example with the word 'jigsaw' the player could dance a little jig for the first syllable, and pretend to saw for the second.

More than one person can take part in a charade. With young children it is often better to have at least two. A small party could also be divided into two teams, with each person on one team acting out one clue to the identity of the charade. The team guessing the correct identity in the shortest time wins.

Instead of words, a theme for charades could be chosen, such as nursery rhymes, book titles, films, pop songs or characters from a popular television series.

## OUTDOOR GAMES

### Overpass, Underpass

Divide the players into teams and get each team to form a row. Team members must pass a selection of objects over their heads from the first player to the last in the row. When the object reaches the last player, he returns the objects back between the legs of the players until it reaches the front. For extra fun and confusion, do not wait for one object to return to the front of the line. The object of the game is to get all the objects back to the beginning of the line as fast as possible. Balloons add an extra fun factor, as they float away out of reach.

### Water Race

Divide the players into teams and get each team to form a row. At the head of each row is an empty bucket, with a full bucket of water some distance away. The first member of each team has a plastic mug. Using this, the team must transfer water from the full bucket to the empty one, by running in turn up to the full bucket and bringing back a mug of water. The first team to fill their bucket is the winning one.

### Back To Back Race

All the players are to run in pairs. Each pair faces back to back with arms locked at the elbows. In this way, they have to run to a line and back again, so that one player runs forwards and the other backwards. On the way back, the pair returns with the player who last ran backwards now facing forwards.

### Brick Race

A start and finish line are drawn. At the start line, players line up with two house bricks each. They must stand with one foot on one brick and put the next brick in front of them, then move onto the second brick while balancing, picking up the first and moving that ahead, and so on to the finishing line.

### Tissue and Straw Race

Each team arranges itself in a line. Each team member is given a straw. The team leaders place a tissue over the end of their straw. One end of the straw is in the child's mouth. The child inhales to hold the tissue on the other end of the straw. The child transfers the tissue to the next player, who must inhale through his straw to take the tissue. In the same manner, it is passed along the row. Except at the start of the game, the tissue must not be touched by hand. If the tissue is dropped, the passing must recommence at the front of the line. The first team to finish is the winner.

### Slow Tortoise Race

Bicycles can be used for this race. A start and finish line are drawn. The slowest person in this race is the winner. The children must be well spaced on their bikes so as not to wobble into each other. Everyone starts to ride their bicycle as slowly as possible. The last rider to reach the finishing line is the winner.

This slow-motion race can also be played without bikes, with the children crawling, hopping or skipping instead.

### Tug of War

This is a popular game of strength. You will need a strong rope, at least four metres long. Divide the players equally into two teams. The sturdiest person of each team is chosen to be the 'anchor' at each end of the rope. Draw a line on the ground between each team holding onto the rope and tie a handkerchief to the middle of the rope. The handkerchief should be hanging over the ground line when the tug starts. At the starting signal each team tries to pull the other team across to their side of the line.

### Hot Potato Relay

Divide the players into two equal teams. Each team is given a spoon and a basket. Make two rows of potatoes in front of each team. They should be very well spaced and there should be the same number of

potatoes as there are team members. On the starting signal, the first player runs to the first potato, picks it up with the spoon (no hands are to be used), and carries it back to drop in the basket at the starting line. She then gives the spoon to the next player who runs, picks up the next potato and brings it back to the basket. The first team to get all the potatoes into the basket wins the game.

### Sack Race

Always lots of fun. Each player climbs into a hessian sack and, holding the top of the sack by the hands, must jump, without falling, from the start line to the finish line.

### Drop the Handkerchief

All the players except one form a well-spaced circle facing inwards. The remaining player runs around outside the circle and drops a handkerchief behind one of the players in the circle. Immediately the player discovering the handkerchief must pick up the handkerchief and chase the player who dropped it. If the player who dropped the handkerchief beats the other player back to their place in the circle, then the one who is chasing becomes the next one to drop the handkerchief.

This is a variation of a traditional game called *A Tisket, A Tasket*, in which the player outside calls:

*'A tisket, a tasket, a green and yellow basket.*
*I wrote a letter to my love and on the way I dropped it.*
*I dropped it once, I dropped it twice, I dropped it three times over.*
*One of you has picked it up and put it in your pocket.*
*It wasn't you, it wasn't you, it wasn't you . . . it was YOU!'*

At the last shout of 'YOU!', the chase begins.

### Egg and Spoon Race

An old-time favourite. Each player is given a hard-boiled egg and a spoon. They must hold the egg balanced on the spoon, while running from the starting line to the finishing line. To make this game more complicated for

older children, make it a rule that if they drop their egg they must put it back on the spoon, go back to the starting line and start again.

A variation of this race can be played with each runner holding two spoons, each containing an egg. Potatoes could be substituted for hard-boiled eggs.

### Three-Legged Race

Players are divided into pairs. The right leg of one person is tied with a scarf to the left leg of another runner. A little practice period should be allowed before this race.

### Wheelbarrow Race

Two lines are drawn, a distance apart. The players are divided into pairs. One player gets down on all fours and his partner picks up his feet, making him into a wheelbarrow. The pair run in this way from the start line to the other line; then players reverse positions for the return trip. The fastest pair wins.

### Grandmother's Footsteps

All the players, except one, stand in line with the one chosen to be Grandmother standing some distance away with her back towards them. The players creep forward, but whenever Grandmother quickly turns round they must stand still. If she sees any of them moving, they must return to the starting line again. The first to reach Grandmother becomes the next Grandmother.

Another version of this game is *K-I-N-G Spells KING*. The player who is King calls out:

'K-I-N-G spells KING!' and at the word KING she spins round to look at the advancing children. Any who are seen moving are out, and the first child to successfully reach the King becomes the next King.

# List of Recipes and Games

## GAMES

This edition published in 1995 by Leopard Books
Random House, 20 Vauxhall Bridge Road, London SW1V 2SA

First published in 1990 by Murdoch Books®, a division of Murdoch Magazines Pty Ltd

© Murdoch Books®, 1990

All rights reserved. No part of this publication may be reproduced, stored in any retrieval system or
transmitted in any form or by any means, electronic, mechanical, photocopying, recording or
otherwise without the prior permission of the publisher.

ISBN 0 7529 0088 9

Food stylist: Wendy Berecry
Illustrations: Gaye Chapman
Designer: Robin James
Finished art: Ivy Hansen

Typeset by Savage Type Pty Ltd, Brisbane
Produced by Mandarin Offset, Hong Kong

The publisher thanks Hide 'n' Seek, Military Road, Mosman and Toy World, Oxford Street, Bondi
Junction for their assistance in the photography of the Picnic Party (page 63).

# USEFUL INFORMATION

All recipes are thoroughly tested
using standard metric measuring cups and
spoons. All cup and spoon measurements are
level. We have used eggs with an average weight
of 55 g each in all recipes.

## WEIGHTS AND MEASURES

In this book, metric measures and their imperial equivalents have been rounded out to the nearest figure that is easy to use. Different charts from different authorities vary slightly; the following are the measures we have used consistently throughout our recipes.

### LENGTHS

| Metric | Imperial |
|--------|----------|
| 5 mm | ¼ in |
| 1 cm | ½ in |
| 2 cm | ¾ in |
| 2.5 cm | 1 in |
| 5 cm | 2 in |
| 6 cm | 2½ in |
| 8 cm | 3 in |
| 10 cm | 4 in |
| 12 cm | 5 in |
| 15 cm | 6 in |
| 18 cm | 7 in |
| 20 cm | 8 in |
| 23 cm | 9 in |
| 25 cm | 10 in |
| 28 cm | 11 in |
| 30 cm | 12 in |
| 46 cm | 18 in |
| 50 cm | 20 in |
| 61 cm | 24 in |
| 77 cm | 30 in |

### OVEN TEMPERATURE CHART

|  | C | F | Gas Mark |
|--|---|---|----------|
| Very slow | 120 | 250 | ½ |
| Slow | 150 | 300 | 1–2 |
| Mod. slow | 160 | 325 | 3 |
| Moderate | 180 | 350 | 4 |
| Mod. hot | 190 | 375 | 5–6 |
| Hot | 200 | 400 | 6–7 |
| Very hot | 230 | 450 | 8–9 |

## CUP & SPOON MEASURES

A basic metric cup set consists of 1 cup, ½ cup, ⅓ cup and ¼ cup sizes.
   The basic spoon set comprises 1 tablespoon, 1 teaspoon, ½ teaspoon and ¼ teaspoon.

| | |
|--|--|
| 1 cup | 250 mL / 8 fl oz |
| ½ cup | 125 mL / 4 fl oz |
| ⅓ cup (4 tablespoons) | 80 mL / 2½ fl oz |
| ¼ cup (3 tablespoons) | 60 mL / 2 fl oz |
| 1 tablespoon | 20 mL |
| 1 teaspoon | 5 mL |
| ½ teaspoon | 2.5 mL |
| ¼ teaspoon | 1.25 mL |

### LIQUIDS

| Metric | Imperial |
|--------|----------|
| 30 mL | 1 fl oz |
| 60 mL | 2 fl oz |
| 90 mL | 3 fl oz |
| 100 mL | 3½ fl oz |
| 125 mL | 4 fl oz (½ cup) |
| 155 mL | 5 fl oz |
| 170 mL | 5½ fl oz (⅔ cup) |
| 185 mL | 6 fl oz |
| 200 mL | 6½ fl oz |
| 220 mL | 7 fl oz |
| 250 mL | 8 fl oz (1 cup) |
| 280 mL | 9 fl oz |
| 300 mL | 9½ fl oz |
| 315 mL | 10 fl oz |
| 350 mL | 11 fl oz |
| 375 mL | 12 fl oz |
| 410 mL | 13 fl oz |
| 440 mL | 14 fl oz |
| 470 mL | 15 fl oz |
| 500 mL | 16 fl oz (2 cups) |
| 600 mL | 1 pt (20 fl oz) |
| 750 mL | 1 pt 5 fl oz (3 cups) |
| 1 litre (1000 mL) | 1 pt 12 fl oz (4 cups) |
| 1.5 litres | 2 pt 8 fl oz (6 cups) |

## DRY INGREDIENTS

| Metric | Imperial |
|--------|----------|
| 15 g | ½ oz |
| 30 g | 1 oz |
| 45 g | 1½ oz |
| 60 g | 2 oz |
| 75 g | 2½ oz |
| 90 g | 3 oz |
| 100 g | 3½ oz |
| 125 g | 4 oz |
| 140 g | 4½ oz |
| 155 g | 5 oz |
| 170 g | 5½ oz |
| 185 g | 6 oz |
| 200 g | 6½ oz |
| 220 g | 7 oz |
| 235 g | 7½ oz |
| 250 g | 8 oz |
| 265 g | 8½ oz |
| 280 g | 9 oz |
| 300 g | 9½ oz |
| 315 g | 10 oz |
| 330 g | 10½ oz |
| 350 g | 11 oz |
| 360 g | 11½ oz |
| 375 g | 12 oz |
| 400 g | 12½ oz |
| 410 g | 13 oz |
| 425 g | 13½ oz |
| 440 g | 14 oz |
| 455 g | 14½ oz |
| 470 g | 15 oz |
| 485 g | 15½ oz |
| 500 g | 1 lb (16 oz) |
| 750 g | 1 lb 8 oz |
| 1 kg (1000 g) | 2 lb |
| 1.5 kg | 3 lb |
| 2 kg | 4 lb |
| 2.5 kg | 5 lb |